Start This
Stop That

More praise for *Start This, Stop That*

My friends Jim and Jennifer Cowart offer a simple and practical resource filled with wisdom for church leaders. Skip the theory. These strategies are based on their real life experience leading a healthy, growing church. I highly recommend *Start This, Stop That*.
—Tony Morgan, author, consultant, and leadership coach (Tony MorganLive.com)

Start This, Stop That is a much-needed "how to" book designed to help you take your church to the next level. Jim and Jen Cowart are not mere theorists, but practitioners who have lived out these principles to build a dynamic church that is making a huge impact!
—Steve Stroope, Lead Pastor, Lake Pointe Church, Rockwall, Texas; and author of *Tribal Church*

Jim and Jennifer Cowart's church growth methods are not just good ideas, but tried and true principles that work!
—Ron Sylvia, Lead Pastor, Church @ The Springs, Ocala, Florida

Start This

Stop That

Do the Things That Grow Your Church

Jim Cowart
Jennifer Cowart

Abingdon Press
Nashville

To our children, Alyssa and Josh,
you make life fun.

To our parents,
thanks for modeling a godly life.

To the staff and people of Harvest,
thanks for living the dream with us.

CONTENTS

INTRODUCTION

Churches, like people and organizations, move in cycles. When we get stuck, it is probably time to start doing some new things or stop doing some old things—maybe both. The skills, programs, and systems that take a church to one level will also keep it there and prevent forward movement. Many churches are stuck in cycles that worked for past generations but are not proving effective now.

This book is about church growth and leadership. This is not the only way to do things, but these tools and strategies are working for the church we lead, and we believe they will help you too. Our hope is that you will take these ideas and adapt them for your church situation. We call that "tweaking." There's a saying we have around our church: "Tweak it and make it your own." We want you to do that with the strategies presented in this book.

Let me, Jim, begin by telling you a little of my story. It's not flashy. There is no Damascus Road experience or time spent riding with Hell's Angels. I grew up in a Christian home, for which I am very thankful. At age five, I bowed my little head and asked Jesus into my heart. At seventeen, I answered a call into the ministry. I married the girl of my dreams. We went to seminary. My wife and I took jobs in a local church. We had our first child. Life was good, mostly.

Here was my problem. I wasn't seeing much fruit in my ministry. It seemed I had done all of the right things. I was serving in a church. I was preaching and loving on people—the same people, week after week. I loved these people and they loved me, but sermon after sermon, year after year, the brutal truth was that we were the same. We weren't effectively sharing Christ with people outside our church walls.

I began to question everything, and I slowly developed a holy discontent. I heard about churches in the United States and around the world that were seeing adults make decisions for Christ. They told stories of people maturing in their faith and living sacrificially and obediently. These churches were alive with a sense of urgency about the Great Commandment and the Great Commission. I wanted in on that action! So, I began to pray a very honest prayer. It's a prayer that you may want to borrow, but let me warn you, it is not very dignified or liturgical. It's just a South Georgia boy's desperate and honest cry for help. Here it is:

"Dadgum it! I want to help bring some people to you, too, Jesus!"

That prayer, and what God did with it, changed my life. Since that day, God has led my wife, Jen, and me on a new, tough, exciting, exasperating, wonderful journey that has paved the way for one of the fastest-growing congregations in our country. Since that day, I have seen more than two thousand people accept Christ in our local church. I have been blown away by how God could use someone as ordinary as I am.

I've got great news for you. He wants to use you too!

This book is designed to give you practical tools so that you can see more life change in your church. We want to offer you specific ideas that can revolutionize your effectiveness in reaching and growing people into fully devoted followers of Christ. Your situation is unique, so take the ideas and tweak them to your needs. Jesus charged us, as believers, to go into all the world and make disciples. It's not a suggestion. It's a command. How well are you and your church doing with this? At the end of each short chapter you will find questions to guide small-group discussions as you process the information and apply it in your church. But before we get into the nuts and bolts, let me tell you a little more of my story.

I prayed my "dadgum it" prayer, and then I was consumed. I went to churches where life change was happening. I read. I prayed some more. I began to see people in new ways. I began to think in new ways. How could we reach that older guy in the grocery store? What about that family at my daughter's preschool or the mall or the grocery store? They weren't bad people. They just hadn't discovered the love of God. Jesus and his church simply did not seem relevant in their lives. So I began to ask questions: "What would reach them?" and "What is relevant to them?" and "What music do they listen to?" and "What concerns do they have?" The list went on and on.

Gradually, I became consumed with the dream of planting a congregation that shared the message of Christ in new and engaging ways. I went to bed thinking about it, and I woke up with it. I got excited! (To be clear, this is not a church-planting book. It is a "grow God's kingdom" book. The way I happened to have done that was through a new congregation, but these principles are universal.) Like I said, I became driven by the idea of seeing people's lives change.

However, not everyone shared my passion. As I began to share my dreams with others, I found out that although no one booed, not many cheered, either. I was learning new ministry strategies and seeking to apply them, but I got a lot of "No" and "Not right now" responses. These were good Christian folks, but what I was proposing was different. It was not the way things had been done in the past. I struggled about a year in the land of holy discontent. Then I had a dream.

In my dream, I died. That's bad. But then I went to heaven. Much better. Jesus was standing there. As I approached him, I remember his smile. It was an awesome moment, even in a dream. He laughed and pulled me into a bear hug. He really seemed glad to see me. It was like being reunited with a best friend, only better. Although it's hard to put into words, I felt humble and joyful. Jesus was glad to see me. We talked about my life. The whole atmosphere was electric because of his smile. But then the tone changed. There was a pause in our conversation. His expression went from joy to something more like disappointment. It wasn't anger, but sadness. He looked down for a moment and then into my eyes and said, "Jim, can I ask you something?" I was scared. "Yes, sir," I mumbled. And then he asked me a question that broke my heart and changed my life.

"Why didn't you start that church on earth like I asked you to?" The tone was gentle and straightforward. It was Jesus' expression of pain that I carry with me today. I had let down my Savior.

In my dream, my mind began to race. I began to form my defense. I tried to shift the blame: *They wouldn't let me. I didn't know how. There didn't seem to be enough money.* I didn't say any of those things, but I thought them. Fortunately, as I was about to speak, another thought pushed its way forward: *Shut up, Jim! Don't make excuses.*

Here was Jesus, the Son of God, the Creator of the universe, inviting me to partner with him, and I didn't do it. I didn't do it because I was afraid. I was afraid of failure, of what people might say, and of the unknown. Before I could say anything in my dream, I woke up.

And then I woke Jennifer up.

"You've got to hear this dream I just had!" That dream put fuel on the fire that God had already kindled. Now, my prayer was, "Dadgum it! Jesus, if I can help it, I will not let you down in real life as I did in that dream."

I was changed.

My situation was not. I still had roadblocks. I was still scared, but instead of being afraid of criticism, failure, and rejection, I was more afraid of letting down the King of kings. I began to live for an audience of one.

Don't get me wrong. I'm not a rebel. I didn't go against my denominational authorities (although some say you should). But I became tenacious about living out what God had called me to do. It made me think bigger. It made me think more creatively. It made my heart hurt for God's people. It made me take risks and accept criticism as part of the process.

If you decide to go the next step in partnering with God to see life change, you will probably face all that too. Do it anyway. Go to the mall or a grocery store, and take a look around. Really look at each person. Jesus Christ died for them. He's waiting for you to help reach them. God wants you to love the people in your community, even the difficult ones. I'm talking about really loving them. Get to know their world and their needs in order to share Christ with them.

What's God asking you to do? Into what project has Jesus invited you to partner with him? I can guarantee you it has something to do with the Great Commission.

In 2001, the South Georgia Conference of The United Methodist Church sent Jen and me, with our children, Alyssa and Josh, then ages five and one, to start a new church in Houston County, Georgia. There was no land, no launch team, and no building, but there was a dream. This book is about the lessons we have learned these past eleven years. Tweak them and make them your own.

I hope that you will join us in claiming your county for Christ. We often say at Harvest, "We want to make it hard to get to hell from Houston County."

If you're willing to ask and answer some hard questions . . .

If you're willing to stretch yourself and take a few risks . . .

If you're ready to be more effective in ministry . . .

Turn the page.

LEADERSHIP

This book is about leadership and church growth. We hope you can tell by the title that we intend for it to be very practical, something you can begin to put into practice right away in your church setting. The things we share are working for us in our congregation, Harvest. That being said, while our intent is for the book to be extremely practical, there are some things that are more intangible. While we suggest taking the practical action of starting and stopping, some things you can see and some things you can't. For example, while the whole book is about leadership, this section deals with starting and stopping certain mind-sets, attitudes, and ways of thinking. A mind-set is intangible. These chapters are more cognitive, focusing on the way we think. Many other chapters are more behavioral, dealing with the way we act.

Scientists debate which comes first and which is more influential, thinking or acting. But for the church, both are needed! Sometimes we need to change our thinking. Sometimes we need to change the way we do things. The two are related. Remember, your results happen because of what you do now. We're interested in improving the results.

There is an old story about a farmer who lost his mule. He looked for days but couldn't find him. One day he discovered an old well in a corner of his pasture had caved in. Sure enough, there was his missing mule, twenty feet down. The farmer could tell that the mule had given up on life. His head hung low in despair. Several neighbors came over to take a look and offer advice. (It's not every day you see a mule down a well.) But no one could figure a way to get the old mule out. Finally, someone said, "Well, we can't get him out. Might as well fill in the hole." The farmer hated to do it, but he couldn't think of a better option. The men grabbed shovels and started tossing down loads of dirt. The poor mule just stood there as dirt piled up on his back and began to fill up around his hoofs. This seemed to spark something in the old mule. He shook the dirt off his back, gave a big "hee haw," and stepped on the loose dirt. After a while someone noticed the mule kept repeating the process. Shake it off and step up. Shake it off and step up. And that's what the old mule did, all the way to the top of the well.

Whether you are a staff member, a church board member, or a pastor, don't get overwhelmed. Just pick one or two ideas and try them. You do not have to change everything at once. Get the momentum moving in the right direction. Pick the easiest step and take it. Then take another and build on your success.

Your mind-set is very important. Your attitude makes all the difference. Will you just stand there while others shovel dirt, letting your church get the same results it has always gotten, or will you step up and become the church God wants you to be? Attitudes are hard to measure and describe, but they can make the difference between life and death. Are you ready to shake it off and step up?

1

Stop the Cruise Ship

Go and make disciples of all nations. —Matthew 28:19 NIV

Think of boats. There are all kinds of boats: rowboats, ski boats, fishing boats, speedboats. Every boat is built for some purpose. You could ski behind a rowboat, but not easily. You could row a speedboat, but why would you do that? Every boat works best when it's used for the purpose for which it was designed.

Now imagine that your church is a boat. What kind of boat is it?

What's the first image that comes to mind? You might think of several biblical images, such as a fishing boat for fishers of men, a lifeguard boat to save people, or a sailboat blown by the Spirit. Those are pretty good images for the church. But here's one that is not so healthy: a cruise ship.

Nothing against cruise ships. We love them! Have you ever been on a cruise? From the moment you step on board, it's all about you! You are a valued customer, and the crew is there to make your trip smooth and enjoyable. They work hard to provide quality service and entertainment for you. Everyone is at your beck and call. (We don't even really know what *beck and call* means, but it's awesome!) There's food galore, and if you don't like something, they'll say, "Hey, just send it back; we want you to be happy." They clean your room

5

while you're at the pool and fold your towel into a cool little swan or monkey. There's room service and even buffets at midnight!

Cruises are great because it's all about us. When we step on board, it's like we own the place. On a cruise, everything is designed to please the guest and offer the most comfortable and enjoyable experience possible. Why? Because the staff are nice people? Well, they may be nice, but their primary motivation is to get us to come back and spend more money with their cruise line. A cruise is all about customer enjoyment.

A church was never meant to be a cruise ship.

You can operate as a cruise ship, and many churches have slipped into that, but it's not why Jesus created the church. Many churches try hard to please their members with quality music and programs for the whole family. Pastors and staff act as a crew, offering a smooth and enjoyable experience for the members. There's fun, food, and fellowship, and the entire experience is about taking care of members and their families. Like the goal of a cruise ship, the goal for many churches is to keep the consumer happy.

So what's wrong with that? A lot actually.

It's not your boat. It's not your church. It belongs to Jesus, and he designed it for something else entirely: a rescue mission. It's about him, not you and me. So, here's a more biblical boat image.

Your church should be a battleship.

That's right: an all-hands-on-deck, batten-down-the-hatches, full-speed-ahead, lean, mean, fighting machine. This ship, the church, was built for a specific mission. It's called the Great Commission: "Go and make disciples of all nations, baptizing them in the name of the Father and of the Son and of the Holy Spirit, and teaching them to obey everything I have commanded you" (Matt. 28:19-20 NIV). These are our orders. They come straight from the Commander in Chief, Jesus.

What kind of boat is your church? Are you cruising or rescuing? Has the crew been assigned to a station or given a lounge chair with an umbrella? If your church has turned into a cruise ship, then you have an identity crisis. You are using what Christ intended to be a battleship for a pleasure ride. When you have an identity crisis, you are apt to do all kinds of crazy things in search of who you are.

When I, Jim, was a little kid, my family lived way out in the country in South Georgia. One day my brother and I found a baby deer near our house that had been abandoned by its mother. Well, that was great for us! We loved animals so we adopted the baby deer and named him Clyde, my dad's idea from an old Ray Stevens song. (Google it.)

Clyde was so little that we had to feed him formula from a bottle. Then Mom and Dad had a great idea. Every time we fed Clyde, we rang a little bell. Clyde began to associate the bell with food and would come running when we rang it. We never kept Clyde in a pen. He lived outside, and as he grew, his two best buddies in the world were our little dogs, Lobo and Mutt Mutt. At first we weren't too sure how the dogs and the deer would react to each other. But pretty soon they were doing everything together. Those three animals loved each other!

Now, for you city slickers, when I say we lived in the country, I mean we had to drive forty-five minutes to get to school. Surrounding our home were dirt roads, cornfields, and pine trees. And when I say we had two dogs, I mean good old mutts. These animals had questionable lineage, slept under the house, and ate whatever we had left over.

As Clyde grew, we had great fun together. After he was weaned, he started eating grass like a regular deer, but he also ate table scraps with the dogs and slept under the house with them.

His favorite game was to butt heads with us. Boy against deer. We would line up and charge each other. When he started growing antlers, we found an old football helmet and continued to go head-to-head. It was awesome! Clyde kept some of his deer characteristics; however, since his best buddies were dogs, he started thinking and acting more and more like a dog.

Living so far out in the country, we didn't get much drive-by traffic. One day a man was driving through the country past our house. Now, while Clyde liked to butt heads, Lobo and Mutt Mutt loved to chase the occasional car that came along. They were little dogs and wouldn't know what to do with a car if they caught it, but they barked and charged with great enthusiasm. Well, that day Clyde chased the car too! In retrospect, Clyde was probably just running along with his best buddies and didn't have any interest in the car that was kicking up a tail of dust in front of them. If animals could talk, Clyde might have said, "Why are we chasing this thing again?" Lobo and Mutt Mutt would have barked, "Because this is awesome!"

Clyde was a great deer, but he had a bit of an identity crisis. He thought he was a dog. He ate with dogs. He slept with dogs, and he chased cars with dogs. Barking eluded him, but if he could have, he probably would have.

Clyde's story has a good ending. He loved Lobo and Mutt Mutt, but something happened to him. He grew up. He started taking longer and longer visits into the woods. Sometimes he would be gone for days, then show up again to get table scraps and check on his buddies. Then one day he didn't come back. I like to think he met up with a cute little doe and they settled down and had a family. Somehow he got back to being a deer. That's what God made him to be.

When a church thinks and acts like a cruise ship, it develops an identity crisis. The church is God's battleship, sent into hostile territory on a rescue mission. Instead of *Love Boat*, think *Navy Seals*. Instead of Julie McCoy, think Patton. (If you're under thirty-five, you may want to head to Google again.)

Some people will be afraid to adjust their ship mentality. They'll say, "What if people get mad and leave?" Some will. Not everyone is comfortable with a mission. There will be those who prefer for you to maintain the cruise ship. But Christ did not leave us the option to choose the kind of ship his church will be. His mission is our mission—to reach people with his love. That requires all hands on deck.

Don't be afraid to raise the bar in your church. Don't be afraid to ask for a big commitment. Don't be afraid to become a battleship. I used to think people would run from a battleship church, but to my surprise, they run to it. People want their lives to count. They are attracted to someplace with a clear vision where they can make a difference. Would you rather be a Navy Seal going out on a mission or a sunburned tourist ordering room service every day? It may be easier to sit around all the time, but it doesn't offer meaning or fulfillment.

You were made to be a warrior, not a tourist. Don't contribute to a cruise ship mentality. If you do, you may have some explaining to do to our Commanding Officer one day. Your local church is a battleship. Are you fulfilling your mission? There is a spiritual war going on. There are spiritual POWs being held captive. Jesus says, "Go get them!" You are never going to be completely happy until you are doing what you were designed to do. Sure, take a vacation. Go on a cruise. Enjoy room service, midnight buffets, and towel art. We need times of rest and relaxation, but we need lives of purpose and significance even more!

Members need to know what kind of ship they are boarding. One way that Harvest does this is with a required membership class. Imagine that you think you're getting on a cruise ship, but you accidentally board a battleship! That would be an unpleasant shocker. Be clear about your mission and expectations.

I still think about Clyde every now and then. We sure had fun together. But I'm glad he got over his identity crisis and learned how to be a deer. I also sometimes think about that guy driving by our house that day. Wouldn't it be funny to have been in the car with him as he looked into his rearview mirror and saw two little dogs and a deer chasing him?

QUESTIONS AND THOUGHTS TO CONSIDER

1. Does our church have an identity crisis?

2. What kind of boat are we?

3. What are the costs of becoming a battleship?

4. What are the costs of remaining a cruise ship?

5. What steps can we begin now to move toward a battleship metaphor?

6. What tools can we use to cast the vision of the battleship to our congregation?

2

Start Casting
Clear Vision

Where there is no vision, the people perish. —Proverbs 29:18 KJV

How do you know if you're leading? It's simple. Look behind you. Is anyone following?

When our kids were small, we took a family vacation with some friends to Sea World in Orlando. We had a great time with Shamu! The crowds were pretty big that day, and as we walked up to an outdoor arena for a ski show, people were crowding to get in. There were eight of us in our group, and I, Jim, saw an opening and broke for a good spot down front. "Follow me, guys. I'll get us some good seats," I called back. I moved like a jungle cat. I bobbed. I weaved. Never looking back, I kept my eye on the prize as I pushed and twisted and wiggled myself through the masses in order to lay down my life for the perfect seats. A bit dramatic perhaps, but that's how I felt.

But when I turned around to receive the glowing adoration of my appreciative family, they were not there! In fact, as I scanned the crowd I had just fought my way so bravely through, I saw my whole group already seated about fifteen rows behind me.

"What's going on? I thought you guys were behind me. I've got these great seats!" I called to them. Turns out, I was excited about sitting in the splash zone. My family: not so much.

It slowly began to dawn on me. My family and friends, the people I loved most in this world, the people for whom I had sacrificed and worked hard to secure prime seating, just weren't going to follow me. The ingrates! That really ticked me off! I had to make a decision. Should I stay in the good seat promised land, or go back into the wastelands of the upper deck?

My mind raced. What should I do? Part of me wanted to teach them all a lesson. I could sit down in the prime spot by myself and enjoy the show as they watched in envy. Only, there was no envy. They were happy right where they sat. What good would that do? And why did I come on this vacation anyway? Wasn't it to be with my family and friends? So, I swallowed my pride and took a walk of shame back up the aisle to sit with my family.

I learned an important lesson that day. When no one follows, he who thinks he leads is really only going for a walk! Sometimes, we leaders can get too far in front of the folks we're leading. We haven't taken time to cast vision and share the direction we'd like to lead them. This is a critical error.

You are a leader. Look around your sphere of influence. Who's following you? If you don't see anyone, it doesn't mean that you are not a leader. It may mean that the people who look to you for leadership don't understand where you're headed. It may mean that you have not cast a clear and concise vision for the people to follow. It may even be that you don't know the vision for your church. Let me help you with that in general terms. Jesus laid it out for us; you don't have to vote on it. We know it as the Great Commandment and the Great Commission.

The Great Commandment

"Love the Lord your God with all your heart and with all your soul and with all your mind." This is the first and greatest commandment. And the second is like it: "Love your neighbor as yourself." (Matt.22:37-39 NIV)

The Great Commission

Therefore go and make disciples of all nations, baptizing them in the name of the Father and of the Son and of the Holy Spirit, and teaching them to obey everything I have commanded you. And surely I am with you always, to the very end of the age. (Matt. 28:18-20 NIV)

We have a leadership deficit in our churches today. Pastors say, "The people just won't follow my leadership." The people say, "We just don't have a good leader." A tug-of-war begins or, even worse, a civil war with brother against brother and sister against sister. As we've talked with pastors, we often find that fear of the criticism of a committee or a few vocal people keeps them from leading boldly. Don't fear it; count on it. It's sure to happen. Lead anyway.

The fact is we need great leaders, leaders who not only have vision but also can share it in a clear and compelling way that motivates people to action. Our people are hungry for leaders who will stand up and lead them. They need pastors and leaders to equip them so that they can take on their roles on the battleship in effective and fulfilling ways. It's time to quit stumbling around and boldly lead our people in the battle for souls.

Stay close to Jesus. Stay humble. Stay focused on the Great Commandment, be nice, and lead well. The primary responsibility of leaders is laid out for us in Ephesians 4:11-12 (NLT 1996): "He [Jesus] is the one who gave these gifts to the church: the apostles, the prophets, the evangelists, and the pastors and teachers. Their responsibility is to equip God's people to do his work and build up the church."

The primary responsibility of the pastor is to lead. However, all too often, pastors spend the majority of their time doing hired holy stuff—visiting the sick, counseling the troubled, attending every ministry team meeting, or caring for the building. These are important tasks, but they are tasks that trained laity could do effectively. If the pastor and staff are consumed with these tasks, they have very little energy left for leadership. The biblical model looks like this: pastors cast vision and then train and equip believers. In other words, the pastor and staff are administrators and leaders. The laity do the ministry.

Following this biblical model has many benefits. First, think how much more ministry might happen in your community if every believer becomes engaged in meaningful ways. Second, the pastor and staff are free to lead and train. Third, laity feel fulfilled because they are using their gifts and time in godly ways. It's a win-win-win situation.

Recently, we spent time with a consultant from a church of around 14,000 members. He is a great guy and an exceptional leader. During our time together, he pointed out the need for pastors to leverage their leadership to help key laity stay immersed in the vision and lead the congregation. His practical suggestion was to make it a practice to have lunch with leaders or groups of leaders on a regular basis, the goal being to check on leaders' spiritual growth, hear updates on their ministry teams, and then cast vision for where the church is headed next. We liked that. We like to eat. We love our people—this should work!

So, let's get practical. How do we do this? How do we cast a clear vision? Here are a few suggestions:

- Use the power of the pulpit. Preach the vision. Use examples. Positively paint the picture of what God wants to do in your setting.

- Make a specific ask. Tell people what you want them to do, and create a system to facilitate that process.

- Leverage your influence with other leaders. Take legitimizers in your congregation to lunch, and share the vision with them.

- Use board meetings to cast vision for the future, not just to give reports that review the past.

- Be courageous and lead boldly.

Pastors, your people need a spiritual leader. It's you. Laity, take on the ministry role that God has shaped you to fulfill. It's a good plan.

QUESTIONS AND THOUGHTS TO CONSIDER

1. Do we have a clear and compelling vision?

2. What is our vision?

3. How can we cast vision in smaller settings on a regular basis?

4. Is that vision communicated in ways that attendees understand and can share with others?

5. Would Jesus be pleased with how we are living out the Great Commission and the Great Commandment as a church body?

3

Stop Saying But

Look I am sending you out as sheep among wolves. So be as shrewd as snakes and harmless as doves. —Matthew 10:16 NLT

One of our kids' favorite games is what we call "So/But." Here's how it works. We begin a story with "so," such as, "So, I was going to the greatest toy store ever to buy you a gift, but . . ."

Then one of the kids takes over: "But there was a giant gorilla wearing lipstick that tried to attack me, so . . ."

It's my turn again: "So, I became a ninja warrior and attacked that giant gorilla, but . . ."

Then the kids throw me another obstacle: "But the gorilla had studied karate under Chuck Norris and your ninja warrior skills were of no use, so . . ."

On and on it goes until we overcome all of their obstacles and accomplish the goal.

In ministry you are going to have obstacles. Jesus told us, "In this world you will have trouble. But take heart! I have overcome the world" (John 16:33 NIV). You are going to have obstacles in life. These are your Buts. Some of you have some big Buts in your lives right now: "I'd like to reach out to the unchurched, *but* my

17

congregation doesn't seem to care." "We would love to have a dynamic children's program, *but* no one will volunteer to lead it." On and on it goes. Move past the excuses and change the conjunction. Instead of saying *but*, say *so*. For example, say, "The congregation has not been excited about reaching out to the unchurched, *so* our next sermon series is focused on the Great Commission and what God is calling us to do in our area." The So helps move the congregation past the paralysis caused by the giant, pink-lipstick-wearing gorilla in the room to a stage of problem solving.

As Harvest experienced rapid growth, we had no space to accommodate large numbers of children. We were meeting in a theater and had a limited number of spaces. One weekend we had more than fifty children in one classroom-type setting. At best it was controlled chaos. So, we had to come up with a new way of doing Christian education. The traditional Sunday school setting would not work. Out of necessity, we assessed our options and created what we call the "carpet group system." Instead of having each theater accommodate one group in a classroom-type setting, we put down different-colored carpets and assigned eight to twelve children per carpet with a leader. Using this system, we were able to grow in the same space to handle 250 children at once.

Instead of giving up, when faced with a big But, we kept struggling until we discovered a So. It has worked. In fact, as we designed our new facility, we chose to keep our carpet system. (This decision saved us millions of dollars, by the way.)

All too often, when we encounter obstacles, we are overwhelmed. Instead of facing the obstacle with faith, tenacity, and creativity, we allow the obstacle to win. When Moses led the Hebrew people across the desert to the promised land, do you remember what happened? "This was their report to Moses: 'We arrived in the land you sent us to see, and it is indeed a magnificent country—a land flowing with milk and honey. . . . But the people living there are powerful. . . .' They spread discouraging reports" (Num. 13:27-28, 32 NLT

1996). When ten of the twelve spies faced a significant obstacle, they not only were afraid but also panicked the people. An entire generation missed the promised land because ten spies got stuck on the But. An entire generation missed the blessing God had for them because a few people would not face their obstacle, which basically was fear. Only Caleb and Joshua said, So "if the LORD is pleased with us . . . they are only helpless prey to us! They have no protection. . . . Don't be afraid of them!" (Num. 14:8-9 NLT). When we look beyond the obstacle, we can move in faith.

To be clear: the Buts in your life are real. You have to face them and find ways of dealing with them. There really were giants in Canaan; however, with God's help, Joshua and Caleb led a faithful generation to defeat them. Basically, we have two options as we face the future: fear or faith. An attitude of fear will give in to the obstacles. An attitude of faith will not give up until the obstacle has been overcome.

While consulting with a church in eastern Kentucky, we were presented with a challenge. Children no longer attended the church. Once we did the research, we discovered there were plenty of children in the area, but on Sunday mornings in that particular area, many children helped their parents with crops in the field. It was a relatively poor area, and on the weekend, during daylight hours, the entire family helped bring in the harvest. The church had a real But to face. "We would like to have children in our church, but they are busy on Sunday mornings." We helped them move toward a So: "So, move your programming to a weekday evening, and prepare a meal for the whole family." At first, some of the church folks complained because that was not their usual church time. It seemed an inconvenience to some members. To this pastor's credit, she did it anyway, and it worked.

As you continue through this book, you are sure to encounter many ideas that you would like to implement, but you foresee a roadblock. Don't give in too soon! Some excuses include criticism, lack of support, unenthusiastic leadership, fear, and financial limitations. Cast vision. Pray. Be creative. Struggle through this process, and come up with a way to move past the obstacle in order to achieve more for the kingdom in your area.

We received a call recently from a high school principal who had shared the So/But conjunction with his teachers. He said that through the halls he overheard one teacher complaining that her heat wasn't working: "I'd finish that work, but it's cold in here." Another teacher responded, "So, put on a coat and get it done." It's amazing what a change of conjunction can do to help us open ourselves up to new possibilities and hurdle past what once seemed insurmountable obstacles.

By the way, this is a great principle to teach the people you lead. Encourage them to look for answers: "I was going to read through the Bible this year, but I travel so much that I don't have time. So, I bought an audio version and listened to it instead." Help your people change their lives by shifting their conjunction from But to So.

QUESTIONS AND THOUGHTS TO CONSIDER

1. What are the obstacles we now face?

2. Complete this sentence: I would love to see our church grow, but _____.

3. Complete this sentence: I would love to see our church grow, so _____.

4. How can you help your church make the conjunction shift from But to So?

4

Start Expecting Excellence

If the ax is dull
  and its edge unsharpened,
more strength is needed,
  but skill will bring success. —Ecclesiastes 10:10 NIV

Have you seen any great movies lately? We enjoy going to the theater, and when a movie is great, we tell our friends about it. When a movie is bad, we also tell friends about it. But when it's just okay, we rarely mention it. Good is forgettable. Good is average. Good isn't usually worth mentioning. As Jim Collins states, "Good is the enemy of great."

You probably don't have many bad things happening at your church. Usually, someone steps up to address something really bad. Terrible music, awful preaching, a horrible smell—when something is really bad, we kindly mention it and do what needs to be done to fix it. What's more likely is that you have a lot of things going on that are just okay.

Our dream was for Harvest to have a first-rate children's program. We wanted to hear kids talking about the ministry as they left church and parents talking about it in the grocery store, just as they do with a great movie. We wanted the atmosphere to be creative, engaging, relevant, and biblical. Think Disney or Nickelodeon quality. That's what we had in mind, and that's what the children's team has created. It's awesome! That's the type of excellence we need to bring to every aspect of our churches.

Of course, providing excellence takes more work. Sometimes in the church, we stay average because we're lazy. Our children's team does a good job because of the time spent in preparation. Every Thursday night they come to the church for a practice. They meet together for a dress rehearsal. Storytellers, hosts, technology team, and music leaders meet every week so that when those little people arrive, we are ready to engage. Do we have staff helping them? Yes, we do now. But with more than five hundred children weekly, we have only one full-time children's staff person. More on staffing later.

If a young unchurched family visits your church this weekend, what will the parents and children find? Are you ready for them? Is what you are offering going to pique their interest and leave them excited about coming back? We get no second chances with first-time guests. Here are four areas where we must start expecting excellence and stop accepting average:

1. children's ministry
2. music
3. preaching
4. welcoming atmosphere

If you mess up any of these four, your guests won't be back. Good just won't cut it in these areas.

An older member once told us that everybody can make a noise that is joyful to the Lord. Whether it's a joyful noise to the rest of us depends on talent. She is right. Morning worship music needs to be well rehearsed, upbeat, and in tune. No matter what your style, it's got to be excellent.

Similarly, each week the message has to be dynamic and engaging. It needs to speak biblical truths into people's lives in relevant ways. A great message is about both inspiration and application.

If the preaching in your setting is not great, then work on it. Go to seminars. Hire a preaching coach. But above all, don't settle for okay.

Sometimes we overspiritualize things when we need to sharpen our skills and work harder. Wise King Solomon reminded us,

> If the ax is dull
>   and its edge unsharpened,
> more strength is needed,
>   but skill will bring success. (Eccles. 10:10 NIV)

Sometimes we need more training so that our tools are as sharp as possible. Don't settle for dull tools. The message is too important!

As with the other essentials, a warm and friendly atmosphere overcomes a multitude of shortcomings. Once we visited Christ Community Church in Columbus, Georgia. The church was meeting in an old car dealership, which wasn't in the best part of town. We dropped our infant off in what had once been a salesman's office. The setting was less than ideal, but if we were going to join a church in that area, it would have been the one. They got three out of the four things really right that day. Before we sat down in the worship center, at least twelve people spoke to us, and many stooped to speak directly to our four-year-old daughter, Alyssa, as well. They seemed genuinely glad we were there and were interested in who we were. The message was biblical and engaging, but they got us with our baby. When we went to pick up Josh, the teacher called us by name.

She thanked us for the opportunity to get to know our son. And on the back of his jumper was a sticker that said, "My teacher prayed for me today." It chokes us up just thinking about it. They overcame their obstacles with excellence in the areas that mattered most. Good job!

These four areas of concentration—children's ministry, music, preaching, and welcoming atmosphere—are too important to settle for mediocrity. Keep working on them until your church has a reputation for excellence in these things!

QUESTIONS AND THOUGHTS TO CONSIDER

1. How would an outsider rate our children's ministry?
2. What would others say of the quality and style of our music?
3. Is the preaching relevant and engaging?
4. Do first-time guests feel welcome?
5. What skills do we need to sharpen? How will we do that?

5

Stop Committees

He called his twelve disciples together and began sending
them out two by two. —Mark 6:7 NLT

At Harvest we do not have committees. Not a single one. Instead, we have teams. At first glance it may seem that there is only a subtle difference between a committee and a team, but look closely. Committees usually meet to plan or approve what *should* be done. Teams meet to *do* what needs to be done. Committees are not evil, usually, but they don't have as many benefits as the team approach. Consider moving to a team-based leadership format.

The difference between teams and committees is a difference in attitude and intention. We've served on committees where we sat around, sometimes for a whole weekend, trying to figure out what other people needed to be doing. What a waste of energy. It may work sometimes, but it's a bureaucratic way of approaching the mission of the church. It's not very personal, effective, or biblical.

Teams, on the other hand, are modeled in the book of Acts. You invest your life, spiritual gifts, heart, and abilities in them. Harvest functions with five primary leadership teams:

1. The Executive Staff Team is responsible for the day-to-day operations of the church.

2. The Personnel Team is responsible for assisting the executive staff team with securing staff to fulfill the staff values and vision.

3. The Finance Team is responsible for making sure that money is handled in accountable ways

4. The Land and Building Team is responsible for helping the executive staff team assess physical needs for growth and maintenance of physical plant and assets.

5. The Leadership Team consists of the primary leaders of the major ministry teams throughout the church (greeters, parking, community groups, and so on).

To be considered for a leadership team, a member must meet these basic requirements:

• Have experience serving faithfully in a leadership role on a ministry team.

• Be a tither.

• Be a community group member (that's our term for the small group).

• Possess a positive attitude.

These requirements weed out people who just want to acquire power. We find that the people who serve in these roles not only love the Lord; they also deeply love us, the staff, and our church. These people would be the first to give up a seat to a visitor or clean up after a child who has been sick in the hallway. They are our leaders because they are our best servants.

The people making up these five teams are the leaders of the other ministries in the church. They represent more than 1,100 people who serve weekly in various ways. We try to turn every function of the church into a ministry team, literally:

- scrubbing the toilets: Clean-Up Team
- clearing the walking trail: Landscape Team
- storytelling for preschoolers: Puppet Team
- taking care of computer networking and repair: Information Technology Team
- ensuring safety of staff, church, and children: Security Team
- sorting through trash: Recycling Team
- handing out donuts: Hospitality Team

Benefits of ministry teams include the following:

- Saves money. Take a look at the short list of our ministry teams. Just those ministries alone save us more than $250,000 per year in salaries!
- Creates ownership. When people serve and feel needed, they are "bought in" and begin to refer to their area of ministry with possessive pronouns: *our* nursery team, *our* greeting team, and so on.
- Helps with retention. We allow people to float from team to team until they find the right fit. When they do, they usually serve indefinitely.
- Produces feelings of significance. People want their lives to count for eternity.

- Aids in volunteer recruitment. When people find significance and ownership, they will do the volunteer recruiting for you because they genuinely want others to join what they are enjoying.

- Allows for excellence. By having people serve on only one or possibly two teams, we are able to bring outstanding musicians, technicians, teachers, financial planners, and the like onto teams that we could never afford as consultants.

- Creates enthusiasm. People like to talk about what they are invested in. Get them invested in a team, and they will tell their friends, who may visit, who may accept Christ, who may serve, who may tell their friends, who may visit, and so on.

- Reproduces vision. As team members are trained, they catch the bigger vision. For instance, "We don't just rock babies," a nursery worker was heard to say. "We provide a safe, loving place for parents to leave their children while they meet Jesus." Once they get the vision they pass it along.

- Builds friendships. Serving together for a common purpose creates and strengthens friendships. That in itself is a great reason to organize teams.

- Generates joy. In a world with many challenges, people need positive, fun experiences. Make serving Jesus fun whenever possible.

- Gets people involved. Getting them involved is a primary function of church leadership. Create places for people to serve, even if you think things are covered. When people are needed, they feel valued.

Related to this move from committees to teams, heed this important note: don't vote. In the first ten years of Harvest Church, we took one vote, because our denominational *Book of Discipline* required it, regarding a land and building issue. For every other issue we work from consensus.

Voting creates winners and losers. We don't want anyone in the congregation to feel like a loser. Voting creates a power struggle and can foster a divisive atmosphere. Instead, work together, driven by the vision of living out the Great Commission in your community. Voting has not been an issue for anyone except those people coming from traditional churches, who often want to be in charge. For some reason, those people usually leave pretty quickly.

When decisions need to be made, 90 percent of the time they are best made by the people on the ministry teams. When larger issues arise, they are brought to the attention of the executive staff, who carefully weigh them with the help of the leadership teams. The goal is to look for the best solution for every area of the church and the community. By working together, we have no winners and no losers. We are driven by the common goal, which has been given to us by Christ: love God, love each other, and make disciples.

QUESTIONS AND THOUGHTS TO CONSIDER

1. Do our committees/teams have a clear sense of purpose?

2. How many people are involved in ministry in our church? (At least 50 percent of attendance is a healthy start.)

3. Are the people doing the ministry involved in decision-making processes?

4. Are people involved with key leadership modeling the holy habits of tithing, being in a small group, and serving weekly in ministry?

5. If we could start from scratch, what leadership system would work best in our situation?

P A R T   T W O

WORSHIP

What would it take to stop worship at your church? Organ blows out? Preacher gets sick? Choir doesn't show? Building burns down? The Bible doesn't give a lot of instruction about how we are to worship God. Harvest was mobile for our first seven years, so we know you can have worship without a hymnbook, a choir, or a building. We didn't have much, but worship happened, and people accepted Christ.

Even after a generation, there are still a lot of debates across America about worship style. I hope you aren't having one at your church right now. *Debate* is the nice way of saying it because a debate seems orderly and respectful. But some churches find themselves in a backyard brawl over worship styles: traditional vs. contemporary, band vs. choir, or robe vs. blue jeans. I have a feeling that God is not pleased with our debates.

This part is not about worship style. We don't care what style you use. Whatever you do, worship "in spirit and in truth."

Worship in spirit. This involves your attitude, your heart, and the core of who you are. Remember what Jesus urged us to do: "'You must love the LORD your God with all your heart, all your soul, and all your mind.' This is the first and greatest commandment" (Matt. 22:37-38 NLT).

Worship in truth. This means be real, get honest, don't play games, and don't use rituals to go through the motions of worship.

Isaiah urged us to listen to God's words: "Your celebrations of the new moon and the Sabbath day, and your special days for fasting—even your most pious meetings—are all sinful and false. . . . I hate all your festivals and sacrifices. I cannot stand the sight of them!" (Isa. 1:13-14 NLT 1996).

If yours is a liturgical church, worship with the richness of the liturgy. Light the candles, play the anthem, and recite the affirmation of faith. But do it all in spirit and in truth to God.

If yours is a contemporary church, worship with your blue jeans and band. Use technology, play a video clip, and rock your little hearts out! But do it all in spirit and in truth to God.

Liturgy is not bad, except when it becomes stale and people don't remember the meaning behind the ceremony.

Contemporary is not bad, except when it becomes a show and people focus on goose bumps instead of God.

Although we don't want your building to burn down or your choir not to show, it is good to strip away everything we do that we call worship and say, "Okay, what do we need to do to worship God in spirit and in truth right here and right now?"

6

Start the Party

I was glad when they said to me,
"Let us go to the house of the LORD."—Psalm 122:1 NLT

"Church is boring." You've probably heard this, said this, or thought this at some time. We have.

Perhaps you have heard the story about the guy who didn't want to go to church. The wife is getting ready early on Sunday morning, and she notices her husband is still in bed. "Honey, you better get up. You don't want to be late for church." A grumpy voice responds, "I'm not going to church today." The patient wife asks sweetly, "But why not?" "I'll give you three good reasons why not," the husband replies gruffly. "One, the service is boring. Two, those people are a bunch of hypocrites. And three, I don't like them, and they don't like me."

Still very patiently, the wife counters, "Oh, honey, the service isn't always boring, and not everyone at the church is a hypocrite. I'm sure there are some people who like you. But I've got one more reason for you: you're the pastor. So, get up, buddy boy, you're going to church today!"

It seems crazy to me that church could be boring or irrelevant, but it is sometimes. This is not a modern problem. It's been an issue for thousands of years, even with God! God said, "I hate all your show and pretense—the hypocrisy of your religious festivals and solemn assemblies" (Amos 5:21 NLT).

Hey, when God is sick of your worship services, you've got a problem! How does it come to that? Sometimes religion has replaced a meaningful relationship with God. Perhaps we have fallen into a trap of just going through the motions without real worship even occurring. When routine replaces relevance, we are in trouble.

When we read Psalms, we find great excitement in worship. Singing, shouting, playing music, and dancing are present. Sounds like a party! But sometimes our worship services seem more like a funeral than a party. What's yours like? The similarities between worship and a funeral can be alarming.

At a funeral, people are sad and grieving. They dress up in their nicest clothes to show respect to the departed. There are flowers, sad music, and a somber atmosphere. There is often a special solo followed by the pastor, who reads some scripture and says some nice things about the person who has passed away. The pastor may even be able to work in a humorous story about the dearly departed to lighten things up. There are laughter and tears. You hear things like, "We're going to miss Joe," or "Sally was a good person, and we are all richer for having known her." It's all very serious, orderly, and respectful.

Now think about a weekend worship service. It's often very similar. People show up to the church. Even though no one has died recently, many seem to be sad, even grieving. (Maybe they are sad because they know what's about to take place!) They are usually dressed up in their nicest clothes because they want to show respect to God or because their mom or wife made them. They may not be grieving, but the tone is somber and serious. Children should be still. No laughing. Just sit quietly. It's all very respectful. Boring, but respectful. Someone might sing a solo. Then the pastor stands up, reads some scripture, and says some nice things about the person who has passed away: in this case, Jesus. The pastor may even be able to work in a humorous story about the dearly departed (again, Jesus) to lighten things up. You might hear things like, "Jesus was a good man, and we are all richer people for having known him." It's all very serious, orderly, and respectful.

Of course, that tone is justified. We are a respectable church. We don't want to be out of control or wild. That's just not reverent.

Although we're not suggesting that worship should be a wild party, we believe it should be a celebration. Why? Because Jesus didn't stay dead! Jesus conquered death for us. Sure, being solemn has its place but not all the time. Not if you believe in the resurrection.

A lot of churches know that Jesus is alive, but they don't act like it. They gather week after week, dress up, and meet to pay their respects to Jesus. It's been said that it is a sin for worship to be boring. I agree. God is not boring, and worshiping God should not be, either. It is our responsibility as church leaders to find engaging and relevant methods of sharing Christ.

Here are some worship party planning tips:

- Get a party mentality! Leaders need to be excited to be there and have a sense of purpose and expectation. Show up to thank the one who loves you most.

- Be likable. The messenger is the message. Be friendly first.

- Improve the pace and flow of the service. Keep things moving. Regardless of style, all services can be improved with good pace and flow. Practice transitions, and don't allow unintentional dead time.

- Choose upbeat music. Primarily use music written in major keys.

- Use humor and stories to engage the crowd. Have fun. Smile and laugh.

- Model friendliness and excitement. Excitement is contagious. Leaders start it.
- Have layers of friendly greeters in the parking lot and building. Teach them to smile!
- Communicate for application and not just information.
- Improve the quality of all aspects of the worship service.
- Be sure that the worship is pointed to God and not at those with microphones.

Life is hard. People need a safe place that offers hope, peace, and joy. If your worship services are stiff and boring, loosen up! Don't take yourselves so seriously! The God of the universe invites you and wants you to worship Him, but don't do it halfheartedly. Don't just go through the motions. Start leading and attending worship with passion and enthusiasm!

QUESTIONS AND THOUGHTS TO CONSIDER

1. How would a first-time guest describe our worship service?
2. Do people enter our services with a sense of expectation? If not, how can we change that?
3. Is our worship experience vibrant and enthusiastic?
4. How many first-time professions of faith have we had this month?
5. How could we immediately improve the pace or flow of our service?

7

Stop Communicating for Information

Don't just listen to God's word. You must do what it says. —James 1:22 NLT

What's the goal? It's a question we need to ask, answer, and re-visit often.

> What's the goal of this Administrative Board?
> What's the goal of this Sunday school lesson?
> What's the goal of this meeting?
> What's the goal of this ministry?
> What's the goal of this staff position?
> What's the goal of this song?
> What's the goal of this sermon?

Many times, there is not a clear goal. Therefore, we default to passing along information or going through the motions. How many times have you been in a meeting that largely consisted of giving reports? People need information. But they need more than that. They need application. James 1:22 (NLT) states, "Don't just listen to God's word. You must do what it says."

Consider the last question in the above list. Most sermons aren't great. And that's a shame. Think about it. The Sunday morning sermon is one of the few times in America when people sit politely and listen to someone talk without interruption. Where else does that happen? It's really a great opportunity. It's tragic if people seek hope and answers to the hurts in their lives, but don't find them in the sermon. We're not throwing pastors under the bus. Most of the pastors we know are great people. They love God. They love people, and they really want to make a difference in the world. The motivation, heart, and spirit are there, but there's often a disconnection between information and application.

Most pastors have been trained, formally or by example, to convey information in sermons, staff meetings, and lessons. We communicate content. Here's what happened to Jonah. Here's what happened to Noah. Here's what happened to Paul. Yet the unspoken question in the crowd in every sermon across America is, "So what?" Not in a rude, "that doesn't matter" way, but in an inquisitive way: So, what do I do with that? How does that apply to me? It's a good question and deserves to be answered.

In fact, Paul used a little Greek word repeatedly in his letters of instruction: *hina*. It means "so that." Information was not the goal; the "so what" and the "so that" were. Paul didn't want his readers just to *know* stuff. He wanted them to *do* stuff, so they could really know Jesus and have a new life. Stop preaching just to share information. Start preaching to help people change their lives.

A good friend of mine tells a great story. He and his wife went white-water rafting. Before their trip downriver, their guide gave a safety orientation talk about what to do in case anyone got knocked out of the boat: "Keep your feet up. Stay on your back. Keep your feet pointed downriver. Find the raft, and reach for the extended paddle being offered by me or your fellow rafters."

Everything started out great on their river run. The water was cold. People were laughing. The sun was shining. They were having fun until the wife got knocked out of the boat. She fell out in a dangerous spot on the river. The water was rough, and the current swept her underwater and away from the raft. She was out of control and couldn't get air, and she panicked. The guide was worried too. He leaned as far as he could toward her and extended his paddle for her to grab. He yelled over the sound of the river, "Listen closely! What's the Greek word for paddle?"

What? Of course, the guide didn't say that. He said, "Grab the paddle!"

When my friend's wife was in danger of drowning, she didn't need a three-point pep talk on the historicity and eschatology of the paddle. She didn't need more information. She needed help!

Every week there are people sitting in church, drowning: in debt, in problems, in sin, in life. They don't need a little homily. They need help. The church has been entrusted with the source of hope, the gospel of Jesus Christ. Sometimes as leaders, we are saying the right words. We give correct information, but we don't bring the message to the logical conclusion: application! "Here's what God says about (money, salvation, relationships). Now let's do it, and here's how."

The gospel message doesn't change. It's good news! But we have to share it in ways that people can understand and apply. As the old saying goes, "Put the cookies on the bottom shelf" where everyone can reach them.

So, how do we communicate for application? Here are some suggestions:

FOR PASTORS

1. *Make a clear ask in the sermon.* No one can follow fuzzy directions. Choose your words carefully. Be specific. Be clear. At the end of a message we give an invitation to accept Christ. We often word it something like this: "If you've never stepped across the line and

asked Jesus to be your Savior, we want you to do that today. You don't have to come down front. We're going to lead in a prayer, and you can say the words to God. He'll hear you. Then we want you to check the box on your communication card that says, 'Today, I want to accept Jesus for the first time.' Drop that in the offering basket because we want to send you some next steps. We want to help you grow in your new faith." That's a clear ask. How can you apply that in your situation?

2. *Give specific next steps.* In almost every sermon we offer three or four next steps for the congregation and crowd to apply. No more than that because we don't want it to get complicated. We just want them to do something in response to the message. It may be memorizing one of the primary Scriptures in the message or doing a good deed anonymously. We try to make it specific to the message because the goal is to engage the crowd and answer the question, "So what?" Every week, accepting Christ is one of our next steps at Harvest.

3. *Learn from people who do this well.* Rick Warren has a great seminar called "Preaching for Life Change." Rick's tools can be ordered through www.saddlebackresources.com.

Andy Stanley's book, *Communicating for a Change* (Sisters, Ore.: Multnomah, 2006), helps build application messages. Here's what it looks like and how we use it.

- Me (Start with personal story.)
- We (Explain the shared felt need, the reason for this message.)
- God (Explain what the Scriptures say about subject.)
- You (Explain what to do; application; action steps.)
- We (Explain the preferred future as we apply God's instructions.)

FOR OTHER CHURCH LEADERS

Adapt these same principles to your setting. If you lead meetings, ask yourself questions like these: *What's the goal of this meeting? What do we want people to do from here?* If you are teaching a children's message about Jonah, determine the primary goal. With Jonah, for instance, the goal is not just to convey information about a man and a big fish. It's to teach the principles of obedience and consequence and explain how Jonah's story is also our story when we don't listen to and obey God. It's about application. Answer the "so what" of this story that deals with obedience, running from God, and God's love for people with whom we are uncomfortable.

Good leaders help people apply the eternal truths of the Scriptures to their real-world lives.

QUESTIONS AND THOUGHTS TO CONSIDER

1. Is our communication style primarily informational or applicational?

2. Are people able to apply the weekend message in practical ways?

3. How can we incorporate next steps into weekly sermons?

4. As an example, what would a practical next step have been for last week's message?

5. What tweaks can we make to our meetings to make them more about application than information?

8

Start Using a Ladder

Encourage one another and build each other up.
—1 Thessalonians 5:11 NIV

Ladders are made for climbing higher, but hammers are made for beating things down. Constructive feedback should be more like a ladder and less like a hammer.

Healthy churches create an atmosphere of constructive feedback. We have a friend who likes to say, "Feedback is the breakfast of champions." This guy is the master of feedback. He loves it. And he's good at creating an environment where feedback is a ladder. But that's not the case for most churches. We all flinch a little when someone begins, "Can I give you a little constructive criticism?" We grit our teeth, smile, and say, "Sure." Then we get ready to be hit with a hammer. How constructive is it if we beat people up with our supposedly constructive criticism? Stop doing that.

I, Jim, had a moronic supervisor once. Rather, I guess I should say, I had a supervisor once who blasted me for about ten minutes with what I was doing wrong on the job. I was really getting beaten up. When he finished his list, I just sat there, wounded. I was trying to be mature, listen, and filter what he said. Finally, I asked what he thought I could do to improve. He said (and this is why I called him moronic), "I don't know. I can't think of anything." Well, that's not helpful! That was a hammer. Hammers beat down.

Ladders help you climb to a higher place. Feedback is a ladder that helps your church get better. It offers clear steps to help you improve as a church leader. Its purpose is to build you up, not beat you down and prove you wrong. In your church structure, with staff, boards, and ministry teams, create an atmosphere for constructive feedback. This means creating an environment where feedback is healthy, safe, and really helpful. You are going to develop an atmosphere in your church either way. Make sure it is a culture of ladders instead of hammers.

Ladder	Hammer
Genuinely wants to help	Wants to be right
Thoughtful with specific steps	Tough, with no practical steps
Comes from a trusted friend	Comes from any ol' moron

Currently, we hold four services a weekend at Harvest. After each service, my executive staff and I, a group of four people, sit down and systematically evaluate the service with the goal of making the next one better. We go through a quadrant of four questions that we learned from a coach: What was right? What was wrong? What was missing? What was confusing?

When we first started this process years ago, there was a little trepidation in the room. We didn't have a lot of experience with giving and receiving feedback, especially as a ladder. Most of us had wounds from some hammer experiences, and that's what we associated with feedback. So we started slowly and just stayed nice. Now that we've done this for years we jump in quickly. Everyone in the room knows we are going for the ladder, not the hammer. Here's what a typical feedback session sounds like for us when things are going well:

"Okay, let's talk about the service. What was right?"

"Music was good."

"Really liked how that last song tied everything together."

"Yeah, me too."

"What else was right?"

"Message was good. Good stories. People seemed with you."

"Okay. What else."

"All the teams were in place. Plenty of volunteers. Friendly atmosphere in the lobby."

"How were the pace and flow?"

"Good. We can tighten it up a little, but we had plenty of time. It felt engaging to me."

When the service has problems, elements are missing, or the message is confusing, the conversation sounds like this:

"Okay. What can we tweak to make this service better?"

"Pam's microphone seemed to have problems."

"I know. Already talked with the sound team and they're working on it."

"I'll check with them again right after this meeting."

"Okay, good. How did the story go over?"

"You lost me on the story about the dog. I didn't follow how it connected with your point."

"Really? It makes sense to me, but maybe it doesn't translate. What did you guys think?"

"I didn't get it, either."

"Okay, maybe I'm the only one who gets it. If you guys were lost, the crowd probably was too. I guess I can drop it. I think the message needs a story there, though, and that's the only one I can think of."

"What if you told that story about . . . ?"

We do this process every weekend between worship services. There are just a few voices in the room, every one a trusted friend who understands the difference between a ladder and a hammer. I don't announce to the crowd, "Hey, we're going to meet in my office after the service. If anyone wants to join us to tear my sermon apart, come on in."

Multiply the benefit of this tool. You can use this little quadrant of right/wrong/missing/confusing with every ministry team. Teach other teams to do the same thing with their areas. Worship is just one area to evaluate regularly. Now that we've done it a while, giving and receiving feedback are just part of our DNA and culture. It's not a scary process because we don't just give feedback when something is wrong. We give it every week, and it's always accompanied with what worked well.

Doing ministry can be a hard and lonely experience. It's better to do ministry as a team, especially if the team helps all members grow.

Here are some practical suggestions when giving feedback:

- Be nice. Can't go wrong here. In the church, we need to learn that we can disagree without being disagreeable.
- Ask for feedback, especially if you are the leader in the room. Show that it can be a ladder. Show how to respond when someone makes a suggestion. Don't get defensive. Thank people for their help.
- Think ladder. Check your attitude. Speak only if you really want to help. And even then, don't speak much. Say it once, then zip it up!

- Suggest possible next steps, alternatives, or solutions. Don't point out the problem in someone else if you don't have something tangible to help the person move up the ladder.

- Use gentleness and respect.

- Begin with trusted friends.

- Develop a culture of feedback as a ladder in every layer of your church.

- Use the right/wrong/missing/confusing quadrant micro and macro. Micro applies to small teams. Macro, to the whole church. What are we doing right as a congregation?

- Camp out in the "right." Celebrate what's good every week. Don't jump to problem solving too quickly.

Creating an ongoing atmosphere of feedback leaves people feeling whole, valued, improved, and encouraged.

QUESTIONS AND THOUGHTS TO CONSIDER

1. Is our church more of a ladder or a hammer?

2. Do we use an evaluation process on a regular basis?

3. Is it helpful? Does it leave people wounded?

4. How would our staff characterize our current feedback process?

5. In what areas can we implement the R/W/M/C process this week?

.

9

Stop Speaking Shakespeare

I try to find common ground with everyone,
doing everything I can to save some.
—1 Corinthians 9:22 NLT

Jen likes to watch British sitcoms. She laughs, but I don't get it. English is a funny language, isn't it? I recognize the words the actors are saying, but they don't make sense to me. What are bangers and mash, anyway? Is it something you eat or a local wrestling match?

Somehow in college I found myself in a British literature course. When I looked through the textbook, which weighed about seven pounds, I said, "Oh, no, I can't even understand what these people are saying!" It was English. I could read the words, but I wasn't following. I knew I was in trouble. Then I met our professor, Mr. Bragg. He loved Shakespeare! Every day Mr. Bragg read the play *King Lear* to us in class. Yep, every day, for forty-five minutes. That's what we did. But he didn't just read it. He explained it. He translated it so I could understand what was going on. I actually learned a lot about *King Lear*. I never would have gotten that on my own. I was lost.

When people who are not used to going to church (remember, that's the people you want to reach) come to your worship service, they should experience something they can understand. You want them to feel comfortable and welcomed, not like outsiders. Many times, though, they feel lost. They hear what you're saying, but they're not following.

Years ago I was invited to attend the first Communion service of a friend's daughter at a local Roman Catholic church. It was a big deal. All the little girls looked like miniature brides. You could tell it was a big event in the life of the church and this family. I felt honored to be a part. As a Protestant, however, I was lost during the whole service. They stood up and sat down and said prayers I'd never heard of. I felt like an outsider, and I'd been going to church my whole life. At one point the program listed the Lord's Prayer. Finally, something I knew! As we began the prayer in unison, my voice carried a little more gusto than usual. It was the one thing I recognized, so I was going to say it out loud! But I messed that up, too, because somehow their words were just a little different from the prayer I grew up with.

Put yourself in the shoes of the men and women in your community who didn't grow up in church. They are outsiders. You probably have customs and language and cues that everyone inside the church understands. In fact, they're so common to you, you think everyone knows what you mean and what to do. But they don't. And people don't like to feel stupid or conspicuously out of place.

Listen in on this somewhat exaggerated worship service. I've highlighted some of the insider language and customs. See if you can spot others.

The Greeting and Announcement Time

"Good morning and welcome! As you will note in your *bulletin*, we ask you to please stand at the *appropriate times* as the *acolytes* come forward during the *prelude*. The choir will *process* from the *vestibule* singing a beautiful piece from *Wagner's Concerto in D Minor* . . . *in Latin.*

"Following the *doxology* we will join together in the *pastoral prayer* and the *Gloria Patri.*

"If you are a visitor, please go the *narthex,* and ask an usher for a *visitor's badge* so we can identify who you are.

"Following the *benediction,* the choir will *recess* as we remain seated during the *postlude.*

"During the *offertory,* please mark the appropriate box on the *registration pad* found on the end of your row. Indicate if you would like (a) prayer, (b) visit from the pastor, (c) prayer but no visit from the pastor, (d) visit from the pastor but no prayer, or our special of the week, (e) prayer and visit combo.

"Also, please check the appropriate box if you would like to be (1) baptized (2) sanctified or (3) circumcised. I can't emphasize enough the importance of marking your boxes clearly! Then pass the registration pad down the row (*so everyone can see what you marked*).

"Again, welcome! We are so glad you are here."

Many of our churches are stuck in a previous age, speaking language established by an English king five hundred years ago. Your church doesn't need its own language. Use words that the people in your community will understand.

How do you start?

1. *Look at your order of service with new eyes.* We've even started calling our printed order of service a *program* because people seem more familiar with that term than *bulletin.* Is there language that the average outsider would not understand? Do you use unspoken cues that only insiders know? For example, everyone in the church knows that when Ms. Mabel starts playing the organ, we stand up and sing the doxology.

2. *Simplify your service.* It's amazing how complicated some worship services look on paper. Some bulletins list every little thing that's going to take place, who's going to do it, who wrote the song, and on and on. Keep the service simple and easy to follow.

3. *Don't make people stand up and introduce themselves!* Well-meaning churches across America make a huge mistake every week. In an effort to make their guests feel welcomed, they do just the opposite by asking them to stand up and speak. Let your guests remain anonymous. No one wants to be put on the spot or singled out.

   Recently, I invited someone to Harvest. She said she had a "family church" but didn't attend anywhere very often. She laughed and said, "It's so embarrassing when we do show up. Last time we were there, we walked in, and the pastor said from the pulpit, 'Well, praise the Lord, the Thompson family is with us today!'" His greeting was probably well meaning, but definitely embarrassing.

4. *Be friendly first.* Go out of your way to be nice. Both friendly and unfriendly are contagious. As leaders, set the tone. Be the thermostat, not just the thermometer. Set the temperature in the room; don't just reflect what the temperature is. If the friendliness temperature needs to be turned up in your church, the leaders are the ones who can do it. You'd be amazed how much a simple smile will do. If you want to see how contagious a smile is, try it in a public place. I do this all the time for fun. As you're walking along, make eye contact with someone and give a big, genuine smile. (Forced or faked is creepy.) The response is almost reflexive. Almost everyone smiles back. Try it this weekend in your church.

5. *Want new people.* If you want your church to grow, you have to want new people. I heard someone say once, "I just love my church and the people in it. We're so close, we're just like family. Sometimes I want to stand at the front door and say, 'We're full. No more can come in,' because I'm afraid new people might mess up the closeness that we have." Yikes! I understand that thinking, but again, Yikes!

We can't neglect the Great Commission. Your church is not really *your* church. It belongs to Jesus. I think many people may feel the way that woman did, but I'd never heard it said out loud. Think it through. God wants people who are far from him to come into his family. Don't solicit new families because you need more help in the nursery or more funds to pay down the building debt. Want people because Jesus wants people.

God loves you. He loves the people in your church. He also loves the people in your community who don't know him yet. Will you make a place for those folks?

QUESTIONS AND THOUGHTS TO CONSIDER

1. What insider language do we use?

2. Is our service relevant to someone previously unchurched?

3. Is our program easily understood?

4. Invite a secret shopper (an unchurched person) to check out your service and give feedback.

PART THREE

Money

The way you manage money says a lot about you as a leader. We're talking about you and your money, not the church budget. In fact, the way you handle money is a determining factor in your capacity as a leader. Think that's an overstatement? Consider what Jesus said,

> Unless you are faithful in small matters, you won't be faithful in large ones. If you cheat even a little, you won't be honest with greater responsibilities. And if you are untrustworthy about worldly wealth, who will trust you with the true riches of heaven? And if you are not faithful with other people's money, why should you be trusted with money of your own? (Luke 16:10-12 NLT 1996)

> The master replied, "You wicked and lazy servant! . . . Well, you should at least have put my money into the bank so I could have some interest. Take the money from this servant and give it to the one with the ten bags of gold. To those who use well what they are given, even more will be given, and they will have abundance. But from those who are unfaithful, even what little they have will be taken away." (Matt. 25:26-29 NLT 1996)

Someone once said, "People get funny when you talk about money." It's true. Leaders are not exempt. We often squirm and feel awkward talking about money. But that shouldn't be the case. As a leader, you need to get your head around the whole issue of money. This includes stewardship, living within your means, tithing, spending, and debt.

We used to struggle with teaching on the topic of money. We knew we needed to address it, but we felt uncomfortable doing it. People are often critical of pastors who ask for money, and we didn't want people thinking that we were personally after their paychecks. And like you, we've seen the televangelist scandals in the news. We didn't want to be associated with unbiblical models. In the early years of Harvest, we didn't talk much about money. Finally, though, we were put into a corner. We had been meeting in a movie theater for five years and had outgrown it. We were using all ten theaters in the complex and doing four services between 9:00 and 11:50. (If you've never tried that, it's dicey! People actually stood in line to get into the next service, and at times, the last song of one service was the first song of the next.) We were maxed out and needed room to grow. We needed to buy land and build, and for that we needed money.

So we did what we try to make a habit of doing: learn from others who are smarter than we are. This time we chose Rick Warren. We ordered a financial campaign from Saddleback called "Time to Build." In the campaign materials was a sermon from Rick entitled "The Ministry of Raising Money for God's Work." That message and the pressure to find room for Harvest helped us dig in and get a better theology of money. Consider this excerpt from Rick's sermon:

> It is one of the most important leadership skills you have to learn. If your church is to grow you have to learn to raise money. It is a key responsibility of leadership. Whoever writes the agenda must be able to underwrite the agenda. If you're going to form the vision you also have to be able to fund the vision. . . .
>
> A lot of church leaders have a real hang up about asking people to give. They allow personal insecurities and personal fears to limit the ministry. You don't need to be embarrassed about asking people to give. There's nothing greater than the Kingdom of God. There is no more significant cause than the Church.

Rick's message hit home. Our personal insecurities and fears were distorting our thinking and teaching about money. Looking at the New Testament, we found that timidity was not a characteristic of the early church.

Like us, you have to get your mind around the money issue. Work through the theology so you can get over being timid about money and move to a boldness filled with love. Money is a powerful tool to help accomplish great ministry. Big dreams usually require big financial asks. Don't be ashamed of it. Instead, give people something significant in which to invest.

While consulting, we have discovered that churches usually don't have money problems. They have vision problems. People give to big visions, but they don't tend to want to give big money to maintaining the status quo. Infiltrate and change your community with the love of Jesus Christ. When you are doing those things, or at least trying, then you will remember, "This is not my church. It belongs to Jesus. We are his church and a force in this world."

10

Stop Pledge Campaigns

The purpose of tithing is to teach you always to put God first in your lives.
—Deuteronomy 14:23 TLB

Years ago there was a United Methodist financial campaign called "The Pony Express." It was terrible. (Okay, perhaps some people thought it was awesome. I'm sticking with terrible.) I'm sure the people who came up with this program were very sweet and had good intentions. But I think it accidentally set an unhealthy pattern that many churches still follow today simply because it's the only model they know.

Leaders in the church were chosen to carry "saddle bags" to the ten to fifteen families assigned to them. Their task, such as it was, was to make sure their assigned families filled out pledge cards indicating how much money they intended to give to the church in the next year. That's what was in the saddlebags—the pledge cards. The "riders" continued their route until they had financially accounted for all of their assigned families. The cards were tallied and used to set the church budget for the coming year.

Maybe I'm being too hard on the old Pony Express program. But here's what happened in my home church. People participated because they were good folks, but the very mention of "Pony Express" caused inward groans throughout the congregation. "Oh, no. It can't be that time of year already."

There are a lot of financial campaigns and giving programs. Most are well meaning; some get results. Your church has probably used some of them over the years. Perhaps you've experienced some success with pledge campaigns. So why am I down on this approach? Several reasons.

1. A church tends to talk about money only once a year: when it wants money.
2. This approach doesn't help your people develop healthy giving and spending patterns.
3. It costs more than it's worth, if not in money, then in influence or "chips."

Stop the pattern of talking about money only during an annual campaign. As leaders, if we talk about money only once a year or just in a financial crisis, we're setting ourselves up for failure in the future.

For example, if you take your child to the dentist only once a year and every time he or she goes, the dentist pulls a tooth, guess what? Your child will learn to dread the dentist. Sometimes pastors and church leaders treat the topic of money like that: "Let's go ahead and get it over with. It's painful for all of us. Just hold on and we'll be done with that nasty old money issue until next year."

Instead, start teaching about money throughout the year. Each year, we do at least one and sometimes two message series dealing with money. Each series lasts four to six weeks. We teach about tithing, budgeting, and saving. You might be surprised to learn that Jesus had a lot to say about money.

We also work some aspect of money into a point of a sermon several other times through the year. We talk about it in such a casual and regular way that people know that tithing is an expectation not only of being a church member but also of being a Christ follower.

Several years ago a brand-new Christian from Harvest stopped me, Jim, in the gym. I had just preached about money, and tithing was one of the points. It was obvious that it was a shocking new concept for him.

"Hey, Jim, did I understand you right? God wants me to give back 10 percent of my income to him?" "Yep," I said. "Wow, I went to church some when I was a kid, but I sure don't remember that part. I'm in debt, so I'm not even close to living on 90 percent. Probably closer to 120 percent!"

We talked for a while. I gave him some of the Scriptures about tithing, and at the end of our conversation he said, "I'm not sure how, but I'm going to try it."

A couple of months later, he approached me again, this time excited. "It works! I don't know how it works, but it does. I didn't know how we could give 10 percent, but we just jumped in. We started giving the first 10 percent back to God, then we cut out some of our spending. Now we actually have some money left at the end of the month, and we're starting to save and get out of debt!"

I'm not making this up. Then he said something that really stuck with me: "I guess God's math is different from ours." That's pretty keen insight from a brand-new believer! God's math is nothing like our math because his ways are not our ways.

Money is not really about money, anyway. It's about trusting God with all that you have and all that you are. At Harvest, we rarely do pledge campaigns. The only time we did was to buy land and then to build. Instead, we teach tithing. The benefits far outweigh those of the typical pledge campaign because the emphasis is on God and his place in our lives as opposed to the church budget and funding programs.

Instead of pledge campaigns, we teach God's principles for financial management. Through sermons, seminars, and small groups, we offer practical tools. We also share the Scriptures in order to help people discover the relationship between their handling of money and their dependence on God. In Matthew 6:21 (NIV) Jesus told us, "Where your treasure is, there your heart will be also." The two are closely related.

People need to hear what the Bible has to say about money and how to handle it. The majority of Americans do not do a good job of handling their own finances, and this poor management causes stress and pain in their homes and marriages. In fact, check out these statistics

- One in fifty households has more than $20,000 in credit card debt.[1]
- For every $1.00 earned in the United States, $1.22 is spent.[2]
- In 2006 more than $51 billion of fast food was charged on credit cards.[3]

No wonder people aren't tithing. They are in trouble! Marriages, businesses, and families are being destroyed around us because people don't have a healthy relationship with money. This is a great opportunity for the church to step in and help. Don't be afraid to talk about money. Don't put it off or delegate it to an annual fundraising campaign. Instead, teach God's principles, the first of which is the tithe.

Pledge campaigns usually emphasize the church's need to meet a budget. Tithing emphasizes the individual's love for God. Instead of holding a pledge campaign, we encourage you to initiate a tithe campaign. Give your people a three- or six- month money-back guarantee to try tithing. As the pastor, I stand before my people and ask them to take me and God at our word, and here it is: "God says, 'Test me.' As the pastor, I give you my word that if you will tithe for the next six months in an accountable way, in other words online or by check, if you don't feel at the end of that time God has blessed you, then we will return every dime to you. No questions asked."

This is not a gimmick, but a safety net for people to take a step of faith. We do a tithe challenge about once a year. More than 150 families participated in our most recent challenge. So far, no one has asked for any money back. On average we see an increase in giving of about 17 percent. That's significant! But even more significant are the faith stories that come out of their obedience. God has done some amazing miracles when people stepped out in faith and took him at his word. This creates positive, contagious conversations within our community that far outweigh anything I can preach on the weekend.

In order to live out God's plan for your church, you're going to need money. There is plenty of money in your church. It just may still be in your people's wallets. Your goal is not just to meet the budget; it's to teach God's principles. If you have been stuck in the pledge campaign grind, consider moving to a simpler process. The process that God established is the tithe.

By the way, leaders, this is an area where you must lead by example. If you and the key leaders of your church are not tithing, you need to get that straight right away or step out of leadership until you do. Our people need to learn about godly principles, but even more than that, they need to see them lived out well. It should begin with you.

As a side note, we have been surprised at the numbers of people who make first-time decisions for Christ during financial sermons. No other topical message series has touched more lives for the kingdom than money. Why? We don't know for sure. However, we suspect it has something to do with starting where people are hurting and discussing who is really in charge in the first place.

QUESTIONS AND THOUGHTS TO CONSIDER

1. When and how often do we talk about money at our church?

2. How would the benefits of teaching the tithe outweigh having an annual pledge campaign?

3. Do you tithe? Why or why not? What about the staff and leaders of your church?

4. Is debt management an issue in your life?

5. Is tithing an expectation of church leadership?

NOTES

1. Liz Zulani, "A Dozen Alarming Consumer Debt Statistics," *Economy Watch* (May 21, 2011). See http://www.economywatch.com/economy-business-and-finance-news/a-dozen-alarming-consumer-debt-statistics.21-05.html.

2. Colorado Society of Certified Public Accountants, "Financial Literacy." See http://www.cocpa.org.

3. See Zulani.

On the next page, see our tithing letter.

Hey ,

Jim here. I am proud of you for stepping up to do the **"6 Month Tithe Challenge"**! You may have mixed feelings at this moment. "How can we do this?" or "Why did I check that box?" Don't panic. This is going to be good. Here's a good verse to memorize.

"The purpose of tithing is to teach you to always put God first place in your life."
Deuteronomy 14:23 (LB)

If you have a significant amount of debt you probably want to start with the **"10-10-10-70" Plan**. This is a simple rule of thumb that has helped many people get control of their finances. Here's how that breaks down:

- 10% goes to the Tithe
- 10% goes to savings
- 10% goes to debt reduction
  (Don't incur new debt and make a commitment to get out of debt.)
- 70% goes to enjoy

Don't forget about the other steps we've talked about; as well.
- Know what you <u>earn</u>.　　- Know what you <u>owe</u>.
- Know the <u>goal</u>.　　　　- Know what you <u>spend</u>.
- Know what you <u>own</u>.

To help with discipline and forgetfulness, many people automate their giving with their banks. If you have questions about the different ways to give or any questions about the Tithe Challenge, just give us a call at the office and ask for Executive Director Tom Crawford.

Tithing is an important part of being obedient and managing our money in a way that honors God. I'm proud of you!

Blessings,

Jim Cowart

11

Start Teaching
Money Management

Riches can disappear fast . . .
so watch your business interests closely.
—Proverbs 27:23-24 TLB

Earlier we noted that Americans spend $1.22 for every $1.00 they earn. If you continue with that math for any length of time, you're in a lot of trouble! One of our country's most pressing issues is money and debt management. In fact, money is a major source of conflict in most marriages and businesses. The church has a unique opportunity to help people by sharing God's financial principles. However, many people expect pressure, not help, from the church. In general, the church has been known for asking for money instead of helping people manage it. We need to turn that around.

Money is one of the most frequently mentioned subjects in the Bible. Jesus talked a lot about it. But he doesn't just say give, give, give. Passages and principles in the Scriptures teach practical aspects of money management. It's not secret or mysterious information. It can be summed up simply: work hard; save; tithe; and don't spend more than you make. That's it. It's simple, but not easy.

Developing a church-wide strategy to help your people with their finances will have a trifold benefit:

1. It will help your people get out of debt and honor God.
2. It will help the church reap the rewards of tithing and generosity.
3. It will be a witness in the world of how God's principles work.

First, preach God's principles. Use the power of the pulpit to provide practical steps for managing personal financial situations. Rick Warren has some great sermon series on the subject at saddle backresources.com. If you'd like to develop your own series, here are two tools we have used that may help you get started.

THE DETERMINATION STRATEGY

This strategy identifies a step-by-step plan for walking through the entire process of money management. There are five parts to the plan:

*   Determine what you earn: salaries, investments, and other income.
*   Determine what you own: house, car, and appreciating assets.
*   Determine what you owe: leveraged debt, consumer debt, and monthly expenses.
*   Determine what you spend: record everything and keep receipts for at least a month.
*   Determine your goal: honor God with all he entrusts in the following ways:
    1. Pay those you owe—debt reduction and management.
    2. Spend on purpose—budgeting.

3. Save for a crisis and the future.

4. Obey God with the tithe—the first 10 percent.

5. Live generously beyond the tithe to generous giving.

THE 10-10-80 FINANCIAL PLAN

The 10-10-80 plan is a basic tool for assessing your financial picture. There are two strategic options, depending on your debt load:

For Those with No Debt	
10%	Tithe
10%	Save
80%	Live on

For Those Needing to Pay Off Debt	
10%	Tithe
10%	Save
10%	Pay down debt
70%	Live on

Addressing financial management in smaller groups allows people to be specific with their needs and develop relationships with other people in similar situations. For several years, we've offered different small-group opportunities to help people with financial planning. Most often, the curriculum we use is Dave Ramsey's Financial Peace University (FPU). It is a biblically based, systematic approach with sound financial principles.

Because financial management has been such an overwhelming need in our community, we recently decided to offer this on a larger scale. We set a date, ordered curriculum, and put up billboards inviting the community. Hundreds of people showed up! Many people who attended did not have a church home. It's a great way to help the people in your church family and those who have not yet become a part of the family.

Stories that follow a preaching series or a small-group session on money are miraculous. Malachi 3:10 (NLT) states, "Bring all the tithes into the storehouse. . . . [God says,] 'I will pour out a blessing so great you won't have enough room to take it in! Try it! Put me to the test!'" When people begin to honor God with their tithes, amazing things happen, and it is a powerful testimony of God's faithfulness.

A wonderful benefit to helping people manage their money according to God's principles is that God's principles bring blessings. As your people honor God with their finances, he will bless them. As he blesses them, they in turn, are thankful and tend to be much more generous. Everybody wins when God is honored.

Now consider these personal financial principles as the church body. As the church, we, too, need to work hard, save, tithe to missions, and not spend more than we bring in. It doesn't matter what the church budget is; if you don't have it, don't spend it. Again, we, as leaders, have to live by the principles we teach.

What reputation does your church have when it comes to money? Are you known for your commitment to help your people manage what God has given them? Are you a generous church, giving to those in need? Do you spend wisely and save for the future? Or are you known for needing and asking for more? It's not wrong to share needs or even ask for money within the church family. But if money is discussed only as part of a campaign, people are going to dread it.

In the past few years most churches have felt financial pressures. At Harvest, I'm thankful to say that we have not experienced the recession as drastically as some communities. Yet it has been a time to tighten our belts. So, we did. We cut back in our print quantities, we reduced the refreshments served on the weekend, and we withheld raises until the church budget was in a better position. These weren't penalties; they were just realities. We found that when we asked the staff and key leaders to tighten things up, we saved a lot of money very quickly.

As a church, we modeled what the average family needs to do when times are tight. Spend less. Reexamine every expense, and find ways to do things less expensively.

Now, we can't just preach this stuff once a year and think our work in this area is done. It's a good start, but set realistic expectations. For these principles to work, they have to become part of the culture of your church. To change a habit, you need repetition and consistency. Preach it. Teach it. Model it. Provide examples. Help your people take baby steps. Help them manage their lives by giving them tools to manage their money.

QUESTIONS AND THOUGHTS TO CONSIDER

1. How have we helped our people with their financial planning this year?

2. When was our last sermon series about God's financial plans? Was it clear and compelling?

3. Who is suffering financially in our congregation? How can we help?

4. How can we reach out to our community and offer godly financial advice?

5. How is our church doing financially?

   ❖ What do we owe?

   ❖ What do we own?

   ❖ What do we spend?

   ❖ Where does it go?

   ❖ What is our goal?

12

Stop Wasting Influence

Choose a good reputation over great riches;
being held in high esteem is better than silver or gold.
—Proverbs 22:1 NLT

As a leader, you have influence. One of the arts of leadership is learning to use influence carefully to accomplish the most good for the kingdom. If you accidentally waste it, you're in trouble. Once it is gone, it doesn't return quickly.

We don't know where we picked up the terminology *chips*, but it means influence. Every church leader, clergy and lay, has a certain amount of intangible influence chips. When you want to influence the direction or decision of your people, you cash in some of your chips. The goal is to continually build chips with people by helping them and spend your chips intentionally in ways that maximize ministry efforts.

Using programs and gimmicks that pester people about giving can be a long process and cost you a great deal in chips. It can cost much more than it is worth if you're not very careful. All leadership issues revolve around influence, but none can deplete your chips as quickly as money. So, how do we maximize influence without wasting it?

BUILD CHIPS BY HELPING PEOPLE

When you help people apply God's principles and those principles make their lives better, you grow in leadership influence. When you teach people to tithe, save, get out of debt, and live within their means, their stress is reduced, and marriages and families are saved. That's a win-win! The people under your care truly benefit, and it helps increase your leadership influence as well.

That sounds nice, right? Help people and become the hero. But good leadership is not always so cut and dried. Good leaders also lead when it's tough, when there is no applause or thanks. Leaders help people go into unfamiliar territory, and that's scary. When we lead into the unknown, we ask people to follow us. Some asks are small. Some are big.

USE CHIPS TO MAKE THE BIG ASK

The bigger the ask, the more chips you deplete from your leadership bank. People will follow you because you have influence, but only so far. How far they follow depends on the amount of chips you have with them. If you ever run out of chips, you're in a lot of trouble because you really aren't the leader anymore. Your influence is diminished.

So, when it comes to raising money in the church, don't waste your chips. If you ask people to do something (like give to a pledge campaign) that has no value to them and limited value to the church, they will probably still do it, at least for a while, because you are a leader. But it will cost you chips. You're going to have to use chips as a leader, but be careful how you use them. Ask yourself, *Is this ask worth the chips it's going to cost me?*

For us, asking people to pledge to an annual campaign is a waste of chips. It's just not worth the cost. We would much rather help build people's lives and then use our chips to make a bigger ask, such as to step up to tithing. It's part of the biblical model for money management and has huge returns for your people and the church.

QUESTIONS AND THOUGHTS TO CONSIDER

1. How can we incorporate FPU or the equivalent in our church?

2. How many families in our church tithe?

3. What do you think would happen if we organized a "Tithe Challenge"?

13

Start Quarterly Financial Statements

*Now I will write about the collection of
money for God's people.*
—1 Corinthians 16:1 NCV

Quarterly financial statements are a great tool. This small addition has really helped Harvest financially. Every year churches are required to send out an end-of-the-year giving statement for IRS purposes. Instead of doing it once a year, do it quarterly. This may send your financial staff persons into a frenzy, but it's really not bad. And once you put a simple system in place, there are multiple benefits. Consider that quarterly financial statements do the following:

GENERATE MORE MONEY FOR MINISTRY

Sending quarterly financial statements brings more money into the church because people are reminded on a regular basis, as opposed to once a year and after the fact, of how much they've given. A lot of conversations in December sound like this: "Honey, here's our financial statement from the church. Is this all we gave this year? I thought we took that Tithe Challenge. I thought you were doing it. Well, there's no way we can catch up now. Maybe next year we'll do better." Quarterly statements help people stay on track with their giving.

HELP MAINTAIN ACCURATE RECORDS

With each statement we say, "This is our record of your giving. If your records are different, please call or e-mail the church office." This is not a letter asking for money. It's a financial statement of giving that helps your people.

CONNECT THE DOTS
BETWEEN MONEY AND MINISTRY

Average church members probably don't have a realistic appreciation for what it takes, financially, to keep your church up and running. It is just not on their radar. When we send out quarterly statements, we include a letter from our executive director that celebrates the ministries we have been able to accomplish so far in the year. We share items such as how many people have accepted Christ, give an update on the kids in the mission home we sponsor in El Salvador, and tell about the big youth event that was successful. We thank them for being a part of the ministries at Harvest and show that giving to the church is a good investment. It isn't long. It is just a one-page letter that focuses on the positive. Celebrating these accomplishments and thanking our people for being a part of them help our people connect the dots that link money and ministry.

CAST VISION

In the same one-page letter that lists the celebration of ministries, we take the opportunity to cast a little vision. Celebration is about where you've been. Vision deals with where you're going. A lot of churches have money problems because they have vision problems. If you don't have a God-inspired vision for your church's future, you probably aren't going to attract much money. On the other hand, if you have a big, God-inspired vision, you will see an increase in giving. Don't worry about coming up with a vision. God has one for you because God is still at work in the world and in your community. Isaiah related his experience: "I heard the voice of the Lord saying, 'Whom shall I send? And who will go for us?' And I said, 'Here am I. Send me!'" (Isa. 6:8 NIV). God is still looking for people like that today. The question is, Are you usable? Are you willing to say, "Send me"?

Casting vision is painting a picture of the potential future. Remember the old Polaroid instant cameras? You took a picture, tore off the sheet, and fanned it as it dried. The picture started out fuzzy, then got clearer. You as a leader, as a team of leaders, need to have a clear vision. When it's clear to you, you still have the task of helping the crowd see it. Quarterly statements give you the opportunity to do this more than once a year.

When pastors and lay leaders share a clear, compelling vision that lines up with the Great Commission and the Great Commandment, your church will have fewer money problems. Remember, people don't tend to give to need. People give to vision.

Quarterly statements have had a very positive influence on the giving in our church. We think it will work for your church too. Just make sure the letter doesn't come across as fussy, desperate, or begging for money. That approach repels people. Give people an update on their personal giving, celebrate ministry, and paint the picture of where God is leading.

QUESTIONS AND THOUGHTS TO CONSIDER

1. What would it require to move to quarterly statements as opposed to annual ones?

2. How can we help our people connect the dots between money and ministry?

3. What celebrations would we include in a statement?

PART FOUR

Growth

A few years ago, a friend asked us when we thought Harvest would be big enough: "When are you guys going to quit advertising and adding services? When is it enough?" Our response was that we didn't know how big the church needed to be. That was up to God. But we did know that as long as there were people within driving distance of our campuses who did not know Jesus, we needed to reach out to them.

The same is true in your setting. As Christ followers, we don't get to decide when to stop growing. In the first chapter of Acts, Jesus tells his disciples to go into Jerusalem, Judea, and Samaria and to the ends of the earth in order to reach people and grow the church.

The New Testament church did this so well that one chapter later, Acts 2, records they were adding to their numbers daily. There was a contagious spirit among those first Christians. They were driven with a passion to love others and share Christ in real and life-changing ways. We have that same task today.

Healthy churches—just like healthy children, plants, and animals—grow. Churches often ask, "How can we grow?" Instead, you may need to start by asking, "Why aren't we growing? Where are we unhealthy?" Then address that issue.

Churches cite location, facility, atmosphere, and desire as common reasons for their lack of growth. These may be legitimate. However, all of them can be overcome. This part deals with how to do just that!

14

Start Three Things

You are worried and upset about many things,
but few things are needed.
—Luke 10:41-42 NIV

We encourage every regular attender at Harvest to plug into three things on a weekly basis: worship, a community group, and a ministry team. That's it.

Most churches are busy doing too many things. We have to get back to the primary mission. Hold everything up to the Great Commandment and the Great Commission. If activities in your church don't line up with these core words from Jesus, then time, money, and energy are being poorly spent.

At first glance, overprogramming may seem harmless. What's the harm of a men's softball team or a handbell choir, anyway? Nothing, if people are being won to Christ and are maturing as Christ followers. But if the church is offering programs because they are social outlets or because they have been around for a long time, it is past time to evaluate. You can justify just about any program or activity with the word *fellowship*, but get serious. What's really working? You can do only so many things really well, so choose wisely.

Jim Collins, in his book *Good to Great* (New York: HarperBusiness, 2001), states that "good is the enemy of great." Most of the difficult decisions we have made in ministry, as parents, and in our marriage have been to stop good things in order to get to the great things.

Early at Harvest we started a very successful midweek service called Oasis. It was a large-group Bible study complete with a band and childcare. More than 150 people attended, and then we closed it. Why? Because we accidentally created a competing system, and it was wearing out our primary leadership.

Wanting to offer a first-rate experience at Oasis, we asked our best musicians, who also led on the weekend, to play. Our children's staff had a hard time finding enough childcare workers without asking those who already served on the weekend. We personally felt the strain of preparing for multiple weekend services and a midweek one. We were wearing out our people and ourselves. Of greatest concern, the number of people in our community groups plummeted. People figured, "Well, I'll just go on Wednesdays once or twice a month instead of getting into a small group." We had created a healthy, vibrant program that was hurting our small-group emphasis. So we shut it down!

It was not a popular decision among many of our people. However, when we closed it, we saw an immediate increase of 250 people in small groups and renewed energy in our leaders. It was the right decision.

Since that time we have worked diligently to protect these three fundamental systems:

1. Weekend Worship

2. Community Groups

3. Ministry Teams

Through these three systems, our people live out the Great Commandment and the Great Commission. We encourage them to focus their energies in these three areas. It's easily communicated and focuses on the big issues. The added bonus is that once people engage in worship, small groups, and ministry, they tend to be committed with responsibilities and relationships.

What do you expect of a "good" church member? In many churches members are expected to attend Sunday school and worship on Sunday morning, and worship again in the evening. Don't forget youth events, board meetings, fellowship dinners on Wednesdays, and possibly choir practice after that. When you add in soccer practices, dance lessons, school events, work commitments, hobbies, and exercise, our good church families become exhausted.

We need to evaluate our focus. Then eliminate overprogramming and competing systems. It's time to simplify what we do; then offer it in a high-quality way.

We've already discussed worship at length so let's examine groups and ministry teams.

SMALL GROUPS

The growing churches we know place a high value on small groups. Most churches believe in groups, but few are committed to being a church *of* groups. Most are content with being a church *with* groups. There's a big difference.

Churches *with* groups offer them as part of a complex menu. For years we served churches driven by programming. The goal was to offer as many things as possible: youth events, confirmation classes, Bible studies, basketball leagues, vacation Bible school, retreats, Boy Scouts, handbell choirs, children's choirs, seniors' groups, book clubs, and so on. The longer the list, the better. Again, none of these activities are bad, but people were so busy with their chosen activity that they didn't have time for application. The church must focus on what the church alone is to do: connect people to God. If you want to be a church *of* groups, you have to commit to focus on doing just a few things in an excellent way.

Take Sunday school, for example, a sacred ministry for many. If Sunday school is effective in your setting, then go for it. However, look closely at it. Sunday school and a first-rate worship experience are often competing systems.

The weekend service is your best opportunity to invite un-churched people into your fellowship. Many churches find that by asking believers to serve on days of worship through ministries like greeting, hospitality, music, children's programming, and parking, they are able to offer a higher-quality worship experience. This is the time for believers to be on the front lines of ministry, not closed off in a classroom for Bible study. The weekend is the time to *be* the Bible study, not sit in one.

Rather than be a church *with* groups, consider becoming a church *of* groups, meeting in homes. This New Testament approach is modeled to us in Acts. Moving the primary time of fellowship and Bible study into homes significantly enriches the discipleship process. Andy Stanley has a great DVD called *From Foyer to Kitchen* (North Point Resources, 2005) that highlights many aspects of group life held in homes.

In churches of groups, youth and adults connect in groups led by laypeople. These groups range in size from six to twenty people and primarily meet in homes. Each group studies a Bible-based curriculum. Each has social functions and mission projects. When a group member is sick or in need, the group takes care of the need. Harvest community groups handle about 90 percent of our membership care!

As of this writing, we have about 2,500 people in our weekend services. About 1,650 people are plugged into a community group. We're working on getting all of our people into a community group. That means we have about 1,650 people caring for one another, studying the Bible together, and taking on local, national, and global missions. We could never personally connect and care for that many people. The staff could never facilitate mission projects for all of them. The good news is, we don't have to because each group does that for itself!

MINISTRY TEAMS

Meaningful service connects your people to Jesus and to each other. When we visited one church, we were introduced to a group of mentally challenged folks who are active in ministry. They serve on a team named after a young man who often asked, "Where is my ministry? What can I do?" He had Down syndrome. Eventually, some in the church developed a baking ministry to provide cookies and cupcakes for the weekend service. Now, dozens of mentally challenged adults volunteer there every week. They love what they are doing, and what they are doing is a blessing to others!

When people find a meaningful place to serve, they not only become connected with others through service but also find significance. Every task in the church can be a ministry. Every believer in your church is a minister—not a pastor—but a minister. It's our task as leaders to help them find their ministry role and equip them to live it out successfully.

Our son, Josh, has been a part of Harvest since day one. He was in diapers when we moved to the area, but just recently, he has become old enough to serve in a ministry. Last year, as we left on a family vacation, Josh was horrified that we would be gone on a Sunday. "How will Harvest work today?" he asked. We assumed he was referring to us, you know, the leaders of the church. Then he said, "The two-year-olds will be so upset when I'm not there to help greet them. What are we going to do?" Here's a twelve-year-old rough-and-tumble football player telling us that we can't go on vacation because the two-year-olds are counting on him. That's awesome!

Being part of a ministry team changes the pronoun for people. After people serve, they begin to say "we" instead of "they" and "I" instead of "you." They begin to solve problems instead of pointing them out and expecting someone else to solve them. They begin to invite people instead of waiting for others to do so. These are changes you want to happen!

Every week about 1,100 volunteers serve on one ministry team or another. Those 1,100 people have ownership. They are investing their hearts and their time in everything from parking cars to changing diapers to folding programs to pouring coffee. Now, if you're a small church, don't let those numbers overwhelm you. We started with two people and grew from there. You can too!

Do three things—worship, community groups, and ministry teams—well. Keep it simple.

QUESTIONS AND THOUGHTS TO CONSIDER

1. What do we expect of a "good" church member?

2. How would our church benefit by emphasizing these three key areas?

3. How many people are plugged into a small group weekly?

4. How many people currently serve on ministry teams weekly?

5. How would having groups during the week enrich our weekend experience?

6. Do we have any competing systems? What can we do to move from competing to cooperative systems?

15

Stop Bottlenecks

You're going to wear yourself out—and the people, too.
This job is too heavy a burden for you to handle all by yourself.
—Exodus 18:18 NLT

A system is a machine you build that works with or without your presence. Think for a moment about the person who owns a McDonald's franchise. Initially, that owner has to oversee everything—the building, the hiring, the cook staff, and so on. But if she hires a capable staff, she can be away from the premises on a regular basis because the systems in place work for her. She will still need to inspect things, but that will not require full-time attention. In fact, if she hires capable people and establishes good systems, she is freed up to start another business and repeat the process. In the end, she will have more free time and more income. This is working smarter, not harder.

This same principle is helpful in organizing and running a healthy church. In churches with systems, all leaders clearly understand their role is not to do the ministry. Leaders are to create and evaluate the systems and recruit, train, and encourage the people in those systems.

Building the system is the toughest part of this process, but it is worth the effort! The beauty of a well-built system is that it frees leaders to move on to new areas of ministry. Ultimately, that allows your church to do more in this world for Christ. Many churches operate through systems, so study them. You won't have to create them all originally. That will save you a lot of time, money, and mistakes. (We love learning from other people's mistakes. Making them ourselves is just so painful.)

Working through systems means that you share leadership with others. Primary leaders will have to give up some of the roles they have assumed and share them with others. What an opportunity to involve new people in ministry and allow them to feel the joy of serving! Visitation and membership care are great places to start your first systems. These allow your church to care for more people and free your staff for more ministries.

Let us give you an example of a simple system here at Harvest. In the weekend service, a communication card alerts the church of needs among the crowd. A ministry team member reviews that information and sends it to the appropriate staff person and the leader of the membership care team. Depending on the need, the membership care team leader then sends it to the leader of the appropriate ministry team (for example, hospital visitation, meals delivery, or prayer team). Volunteers make the visits, deliver the meals, and pray. The care team leader keeps the staff informed about how people are doing. When appropriate, the pastor personally gets involved. In churches of more than one hundred, a pastor who is trying to do all of the membership care personally will limit what can be accomplished. With a system, the possibilities are endless.

Leaders, if there is a job that doesn't get done without you, you are the bottleneck. In fact, if any ministry in your church would not happen when an individual is sick or out of town, you need to build a system. When Moses tried to care for all of the Hebrews in the desert, his father-in-law, Jethro, confronted him and pointed out that his workload was ridiculous. The idea that Moses was the only one in the nation who could judge wisely did not give credit to the other leaders like Joshua and Caleb. How could one man listen to every concern and care for every need? Jethro suggested that Moses work smarter by building a system. That is a valuable lesson for us.

People who have been doing the tasks as individuals are often reluctant to share responsibility. This is a common roadblock to building systems. They sometimes regard sharing the ministry as a demotion. This is a pride issue. If possible, share the vision of systems with them early on. Help leaders see their increased value when they become the trainer, the scheduler, or the encourager for the system. However, if they cannot or will not "get it," move around them. Do not allow them to remain a bottleneck for ministry.

All too often, the primary bottleneck for ministry is the pastor. Sometimes it's the pastor's fault. Other times it's the fault of members and their expectations. At still other times, it's the default way of doing things. Whatever your situation, break out of a bottleneck mentality. Move toward becoming a disciple-making machine that operates through systems.

Every ministry in the church can have a system, even the preaching. Like many churches, Harvest does not have an associate pastor on staff. If Jim wakes up sick on the weekend, then I, Jen, take over. I always review a copy of the preaching notes, just in case. If both of us get sick, the executive director steps up; the next level, if needed, is a lay member of the congregation. That person can get the notes from my capable assistant, who knows where my stuff is better than I do. Now, if by some freak plague we all got sick at the same time, the band would love it because our worship leader would take over and have a wonderful time leading the congregation in an hour of praise music. That's our system, and we've used it on many occasions. However, the band is still waiting for the chance to get the whole service.

While visiting a church years ago, I, Jen, was blown away by the quality and size of the programming for children. I observed a service and watched quietly to see how the staff and volunteers worked. Then I hung back after the service and pulled a key volunteer aside to ask a few questions. I wanted to know, "How does this happen?" As a Christian educator, I heard a surprising answer: "What you're looking for is an administrator who knows how to recruit people and run an Excel spreadsheet."

That was a mind shift for us. Instead of looking for people who were just good with children and loved the Lord, we needed people who also were great at leading others and building a system. That's who we hired, and our ministry grew quickly from 50 to more than 500 children a weekend. It takes 153 people to run our children's ministry every weekend. The staff who oversee them—and we have only one full-time person in that area—interact well with parents and kids. The staff's primary role is to evaluate systems and recruit, train, and encourage people in the system so that ministry continues to be effective and engaging. It works because there is a system in place!

A key in creating a successful system is to think of things backward. In other words, plan with the end in mind. The goal for our children's ministry was to build a system that would:

- handle up to 800 children in a safe atmosphere;
- allow each child to be in a meaningful small-group relationship with a trained leader;
- deliver quality lessons that are relevant, engaging, and biblical.

A system was created that would handle not only the kids we have but also the kids we have not yet met. The system that we put in place for 80 children will continue to work for 800.

A primary system to consider for your church is the small-group system. (As noted, we call them community groups.) A healthy small-group system will aid in teaching the Bible, caring for members' needs, creating mission initiatives, developing friendships, and generating ministry team members.

Additionally, a system of small groups will work even when one or two leaders decide to take a break because someone else in the group steps in to facilitate. Group health is not built on the presence of any single person.

Not everyone is a systems thinker. This may or may not come easily for you. If it doesn't, don't give up. Visit places doing things well and you are sure to find systems there. Find someone to coach you through the process. Perhaps someone in your midst who is already doing this in the secular world could lend his or her expertise to the church.

Building teams and creating systems will reduce burnout because they allow key people to step out of leadership temporarily and rest. The system can continue without them for a while. It also empowers new leaders and gives them a meaningful place to serve. However, the primary benefit of systems is that ministry grows exponentially.

QUESTIONS AND THOUGHTS TO CONSIDER

1. What bottlenecks are we currently facing?

2. If our pastor or any member of the staff was gone for a month, how would we function?

3. What system could we put in place immediately?

16
Start Big Things

You can ask for anything in my name, and I will do it,
so that the Son can bring glory to the Father.
—John 14:13 NLT

If you want to generate positive momentum in your congregation, start a big, new project. Starting a new service, a new outreach ministry, or a building project generates energy and excitement, and that creates momentum. Each of those projects requires serious capital, so let me suggest another place to begin—missions. Ask the Lord to direct your leadership team to a need in the world that you can attack. Beginning a mission-oriented project is rarely criticized, can be done outside the budget, and is a great way to get people to work together. It will also generate buzz outside the church, which piques the interest of unchurched people in your community. Taking on big, noble causes requires faith, and it will keep you seeking the Lord's help every step of the way.

Of course, *big* is a relative term, so select a project that will stretch your particular situation. In smaller churches, that may be building a Habitat for Humanity house. In larger situations, it may be to end slavery in a small country. (We're telling you, we want you to think big!)

In 2011, Harvest partnered with International Justice Mission to bring about a raid on a brothel in India. The project cost forty thousand dollars, which our people raised as part of a Christmas offering. Three months after the money was spent, we received a picture and a story about Salila, one girl who was rescued from that situation. It was exciting, and our people got behind it. In fact, a few of our members were so touched that they now are actively involved at state and national levels to lobby Congress to end slavery worldwide.

Another big project has been to take on the care and sponsorship of orphaned children in Central America. We call this orphanage Harvest Home. Families within our church support these children financially through a monthly sponsorship. Additionally, several times a year a group of the sponsors go to the home to build relationships with the children. It has been an awesome experience for everyone involved! The oldest child at Harvest Home just finished high school, and when members of the church heard about it, they brought us six thousand dollars and said they wanted to be sure that she had the opportunity to attend college or a vocational school. This money will completely cover this young woman's higher education plus a computer. We are not sure who has been blessed more: these children or us.

Our most recent project was to pack the major food pantries in our area. For two weeks in worship, we shared that the pantries were out of food and families were not able to receive needed supplies. Then on the third week we did something about it. We dismissed each service twenty minutes early and asked our members to pick up their children and go directly to one of several grocery stores and buy nonperishable food items. We had many volunteers waiting in the parking lots with trucks ready to receive the food. In twenty-four hours we collected and distributed more than seventeen thousand pounds of food. We were able to stock all of the pantries as promised, and our people got very excited about rushing to the stores to do something for others. On top of that, it was a really fun weekend!

We also encourage each small group to take on a big mission project. The groups that work on mission projects tend to be healthier and more cohesive than those that don't. We lead a community group for middle and high school students every week. Last year we told them about a friend in El Salvador, Jaime, who was trying to start a church in the jungle. The youth asked us to call him so they could hear his story. So, we put him on speakerphone, and through broken English, he shared his dream. To our surprise, after the kids left that evening, there was more than one hundred dollars on our kitchen counter. The students quietly left money there for our friend. Over the next few weeks, the kids continued to bring money until we were able to send Jaime the equivalent of a month's salary. That was from twelve- and thirteen-year-olds. Now, a year later, they still want to hear reports about Jaime in the jungle. They are invested!

If you want to start a project, begin by identifying a need in your area. You may want to call the Department of Family and Children's Services or a food pantry in your community. They will be able to tell you about families in crisis right in your backyard. Research the situation, and then dream big. God is waiting on people to say, "Use me, Lord."

You get the idea. The options are endless because there are so many needs in our world. Dream big, design a system for how the project will function, and then cast the vision to your people and your community. Let it be said of your church that it is actively caring for the least of these in our world in significant ways. That's a great reputation to have, and newspapers and television stations love these stories. It's a great way to get free positive advertising and to let people know that your church is alive and well.

If your church has been stagnant for a while, pray about taking on a big, crazy project. A small one won't get anyone's attention and won't require you to move in faith. So, make it big, work hard, and watch what God will do.

QUESTIONS AND THOUGHTS TO CONSIDER

1. What is our church known for?

2. When was the last time we had a big win?

3. If we could attempt anything, what would it be?

4. What needs are on our radar?

5. How can we begin to dream bigger?

17

Stop Expecting Uninvited Company

Go out into the highways and hedges, and compel them to come in,
that my house may be filled.
—Luke 14:23 NKJV

We bet you would be surprised if we showed up at your house for dinner tonight. How weird would it be for us to swing by your house, plop down at your kitchen table, and say, "How's it going? What's for dinner?" People just don't do that. People rarely come over uninvited.

Architecture reflects culture. Consider how homes have changed over the past few decades. In our parents' and grandparents' day, most houses were built with a front porch. If you didn't grow up with one, you've probably seen black-and-white reruns of *The Andy Griffith Show*, where residents of Mayberry spent their days rocking on the front porch, sipping lemonade, and speaking to people as they walked by. Sounds nice, doesn't it? The pace was slower, and people knew their neighbors.

Fast-forward to the present day. Instead of a front porch, we have a deck in the back of the house. We barbecue back there. We may grow a little garden of upside-down tomato plants. We put up bamboo wind chimes that came with our Ginsu knives. We sit in the sun and relax on the deck. We even have garage doors with automatic openers. This may be the modern-day version of the drawbridge around the castle.

This really isn't a judgment against where we are today or how we construct buildings. As the cliché goes, "It is what it is." The way we interact and socialize has changed. Think about your home. What's your first thought when you hear the doorbell or the phone ring unexpectedly? Do you think, *Oh, goodie, we have drop-in company?* or *I'm so glad someone wants to call and talk to me. Maybe he or she wants to sell me something!* If you do, that's awesome, but you're weird. Just kidding. You're not weird. If you are reading this book, we're sure you are highly intelligent and good-looking. But suffice it to say that most people now regard the doorbell and the telephone as interruptions. Why? They're uninvited.

This perception affects your church.

Even before the movie *Field of Dreams* introduced the concept "If you build it, they will come," that was the attitude of most churches. We are here. Let the people come! And that worked years ago. The church building was once considered a public building. Town hall meetings, neighborhood bazaars, and all kinds of activities centered on the church. It was a place where the community gathered. Not anymore. Now the church is seen as a private club. You don't just show up. The perception is that you need to be a member or to receive an invitation. That's not the image we're going for, but it's the reality in many places.

So what do we do about this cultural shift?

We invite! It's the basic way people come to know Jesus. What's your story? How did you start attending church? Someone probably invited you. Most people come to church because someone invites and then brings them. The church word for this is *evangelism*.

I, Jim, remember preaching a sermon about evangelism a while back. It's one of my favorite subjects, but I must have really been off my game that day. After the service, a Jewish woman who had recently accepted Christ came up to me very distressed and said, "Jim, I just can't do that. I can't."

I didn't know what she was talking about at first. "What do you mean?" I asked.

She said, "This whole thing about evangelism. It makes me so nervous. I just can't do it."

I started laughing because she was one of the best inviters in our church. She had brought in neighbors, friends, and tennis partners. She was warm, friendly, and excited. I said, "I don't know what you heard in the sermon, but you are already doing exactly what I want you to do. You're inviting your friends and family, and you're awesome at that!"

She looked puzzled for a minute, then said, "But I thought evangelism was knocking on strangers' doors and telling them about Jesus."

I asked, "Did you hear me say that?"

"Well, no, but that's what I've always thought it was, and I can't do that."

I said, "I guess that's one form of evangelism, but I don't think it's very effective. I know I wouldn't respond well to a stranger. I just want you to keep inviting your family and friends."

Her face lit up with a smile of relief, and she declared, "Well, I can do that!"

Exactly. You and your people can too.

If you or your church balks at evangelism because it sounds like "knocking on doors," you've got to help people think about it from different angles. It's marketing. It's advertising. But at its essence, evangelism is sharing good news. It's inviting. And there is nothing as powerful as a personal invitation. That's good news for the local church because that means the most cost-efficient method of evangelism is also the most effective method.

We do a good bit of advertising to invite people to Harvest. We use billboards and bulk mailers. We've tried radio, television, and newspapers. But nothing replaces the personal invitation. I tell my people that. When we are getting ready to advertise for a big event like Easter, I tell my people that this is to supplement and help them invite: "Hey, I want you to come with me to church on Easter. We go to Harvest." "Oh, yeah. Is that the billboard? I think I got something in the mail from that church too. We've been thinking about trying it."

Consider these techniques:

INVITE THROUGH ADVERTISING

If you can afford it, experiment with different forms of media. Find out what works in your area. But always make your advertising an invitation. Sometimes churches make the mistake of just listing the event or times and services. That's the same attitude as, "If we build it, they will come." Don't just tell the community where you are or how great you are. Invite them to come and see. Let them know that you want them to visit.

To determine what will work in your area, contact local marketing firms and ask. Direct mail, television, radio, Facebook, QR codes, and billboards have worked for us, but you have to learn your community to know how to invest strategically and wisely in advertising.

GIVE YOUR PEOPLE INVITATIONAL TOOLS

Equipping your people with invitational tools empowers them to do the inviting. The people in your church are potentially your most powerful form of invitation. We say potentially because many churches have not activated their members as an invitation force. They are just sitting there with great, latent potential.

You, as the leader, need to ask them to invite, model it for them, and equip them to do it. When you can put something in their hands, it will help them take the next step of inviting.

Periodically, we print up cards for our people to share with others. Sometimes these are business-card size, and other times, when we send out postcard mailers, we have extras printed to give to our people. We'll say, "Would you take this little card and check it out? It's not to stick on your refrigerator. We want you to use this card to invite one of your friends to Harvest this week. Now, don't give it to your buddy who goes to the Baptist church across town. He's already going to heaven. Give it to somebody you know who doesn't go to church."

Another little tool to give away is pens. Every week we use an outline with the weekend message, and since there are some fill-in-the-blanks, we also have pens available. The pens have our logo and website on them. Every once in a while we'll say, "Okay, guys, today is Pen Day. Here's what we want you to do. When you leave this service, we want each of you to take a pen with you. But don't take it home and stick it in the kitchen drawer. Today, when you go out to eat and sign your check, give your pen to your server, and invite him or her to Harvest. Or take it to work tomorrow, and give it to a friend with an invitation to join you next week at worship."

Tell people in a clear and friendly way what you want. (Invite.) Model how you want them to do it. (Give an example.) And give them a little tool. (Hand out a card or pen.)

ASK PEOPLE TO INVITE

We often do this leading up to a big day like Easter. I'll say something like, "Today on your communication card, I want you to give us the first names of three people you are going to invite for Easter. All we need is their first names, not their addresses or phone numbers, because we aren't going to invite them. You are. You have a relationship and friendship with them. Here's how the church staff is going to partner with you; we're going to pray for you and your friends this week as you invite them."

HOST SPECIAL EVENTS

Your people need something cool and interesting to which to invite their friends. You know your area and your people. What do they think cool and interesting would be? It all depends on where you live and who lives within driving distance of your church. For some churches, it may be a concert or a financial planning course. For others, it's a tractor pull! At Harvest we have hosted picnics, concerts, special speakers, and barbecues.

You can also turn your weekend messages into interesting topics that will appeal to the community. For example, these are series topics that we have advertised in hopes of drawing people who don't yet have a church home:

- Raising Great Kids
- Affair Proofing Your Marriage
- How to Get Out of Debt
- Supernatural
- God on Your iPod

You get the idea. People are waiting for an invitation to come to your church.

Recently, we saw a guy walk up to our church with one of our invitations in his hand. We had just done a big bulk mailer, and he was carrying it like an admission ticket. He talked with one of our greeters and then walked into the lobby. New people usually come when we do a big mailer, but we'd never seen anyone bring the mailer with him. This was curious, so we asked the greeter what he said.

The greeter was a little choked up and had to get her breath. She finally spoke: "He said, 'Your church sent this invitation to me in the mail. Is it okay if I come in?'"

Start inviting.

Business-sized cards can be ordered from a local source or a print-service website such as Vistaprint.com. They cost about twenty-five dollars for five hundred cards and are a glossy high-quality tool. Gettyimages.com has thousands of free images you can use to design your card. It's simple.

Mailer cards, like the one below, can be ordered through various sources including Outreach.com. However, most local print shops can produce a high-quality mailer and may even provide bulk mail service. This particular card was designed in-house and handed out to our people to use as invitations as well as being mailed to the community. The actual size is that of a large postcard.

QUESTIONS AND THOUGHTS TO CONSIDER

1. Has your congregation been trained and challenged to invite constantly?

2. What cool and interesting event could you offer to your community?

3. Why not try it?

4. What tools can you provide this month to equip your people as inviters?

18

Stop Holy Huddles

God our savior . . . wants all people to be saved and
to come to a knowledge of the truth.
—1 Timothy 2:3-4 CEB

For several years we hosted a community-wide dodgeball event for teenagers. We advertised it well, and hundreds of kids participated. The winners got cool prizes, and everyone had a great time. It seemed like a huge success, but we began to notice that very few of the new kids had gotten involved in our student community groups or come back for worship.

So, in keeping with our earlier principle to stop saying but and start saying so, we tried something new. We had the tournament on a Saturday afternoon, and before the finals were played, we invited everyone into the worship center for our weekly Saturday service. It was smelly; it was loud; and it was fun. Best of all, about twenty of those kids joined a community group the next week. By attending the service and meeting some of our leaders, they became connected.

One way to grow your church is to invite your community to special events held in conjunction with your weekend service. There are three elements to this:

1. Invite the community to an event that piques their interest.
2. Make sure the quality is outstanding.
3. Offer it in conjunction with the regular weekend service.

Get to know your community, especially people who are not in a church. What are their interests? For instance, we have found that almost every young family, whether or not they celebrate Easter, want their children to have an egg hunt experience. Therefore, we offer one that is open to everyone in the community. And we make sure it is huge! Every child is able to walk away with eggs galore. We don't even pay for the eggs. We ask attendees to bring sealed eggs filled with wrapped candy. We end up with tens of thousands of eggs, and it doesn't cost the church anything. People like to participate, even if they do not have children at home. That's the first step: invite the community to something that piques their interest.

The second step is to make sure you "wow" them. When we do community events, they have to be billboard worthy. In other words, if we are going to do something, we want to do it well enough and big enough that it warrants renting billboards to spread the word. If it's not worth that, it's probably not worth doing. With that kind of big thinking you generate a sense of energy and excellence.

The third step is to drive these events toward your worship service. Your worship experience is your front door. By combining special events and the worship service, you help people gain a real sense of who you are as a church. They can see the pastor, get a feel for your style, and have a chance to evaluate whether they could see themselves fitting in. This is critical for a return visit.

Combining these three elements creates a turbo boost of growth for your church. For years we held our community-wide egg hunt the Saturday morning before Easter. Hundreds of people attended, but almost none of them came back for the Easter service. Then we decided to have the Easter egg hunt following our services. Attendance doubled! Our worship attendance also doubled, which led to double-digit first-time professions of faith.

For several years we hosted the African Children's Choir. We advertised the event for a Thursday evening, and several hundred people attended. Dozens of these people were African Americans who did not usually attend our church. It was all very nice, but of the new people who came, none returned for weekend services. They had simply been guests at a concert. So, just as we had done with the dodgeball event, we decided to invite the choir to perform fewer songs in conjunction with our regular service times. Our band did two songs. The sermon lasted about fifteen minutes, and then we turned it over to the choir. Instead of offering our community an interesting program, we offered them a dynamic peek into our worship experience. Fifteen hundred people attended, and we saw a 14 percent increase in regular attendance the next weekend. In addition, several people accepted Christ. Most guests came because of the African Children's Choir, but they came back because they found the worship experience engaging.

We now drive almost all of our events to a service. For instance, baptisms are done following the Saturday service. People being baptized invite their friends and family, many of whom are not Christians, to come for the service and their baptism as opposed to just a baptism service. On these nights, there is often a dramatic increase in professions of faith, and usually, a few of the friends and family return for worship the next week. Special events for youth and children are conducted prior to or within regular worship. We strive to make these events so engaging that the guests become regular attenders, who then become fully involved members growing in Jesus.

Most churches are doing too many things, and many of those things are designed to keep those already in the pews happy. The people already in your church are already going to heaven. Sure we need to love on them, nurture them, and enjoy life together. But we should exert our best energies on reaching people who are not yet part of God's family. To do this, we need to be selective in what we offer our community. Let it be said of your church that when you do something, you do it very well. Once you decide to do a special event, make it billboard worthy, and drive it to your service. You are sure to see immediate results in the form of new believers and larger numbers in worship.

QUESTIONS AND THOUGHTS TO CONSIDER

1. What are the interests of the people in our community?

2. What felt needs do they share (debt, parenting, marriage, career, stress, loneliness)?

3. In the past six months what have we done to invite the community into our services?

4. Do we invite people to "billboard worthy" events?

5. What "billboard worthy" event could we host in conjunction with a worship service in the next three months?

19

Stop the
Trickle-Away Effect

Be wise in the way you act toward outsiders;
make the most of every opportunity.
—Colossians 4:5 NIV

In the last few chapters, we've addressed the need to invite guests into the church. Let's assume you get them there. What happens next? When visitors are on your campus, you need a clear process to assimilate them into your church family. As Paul instructed, we have to be wise in the way we act and make the absolute most of every opportunity we are given. In other words, you've got one shot to make a great first impression, so don't waste it.

Most people will decide in the first seven minutes on your campus whether they will come back. That means, in most cases, before they ever see the pastor or hear a song, they have made up their minds about what they're going to do. Therefore, where they park, how they're greeted, the cleanliness of the facility, and the childcare process become vitally important in making a strong first impression. Go the extra mile to be sure those processes are polished and accommodating for people who don't yet call your church home.

113

Consider your greeting ministry. Now we're not talking about a greeting from the pulpit, but a warm welcome as they park, as they enter the building, and as they look for refreshments, bathrooms, children's rooms, and so on. This should be done in several friendly layers. Our goal is that every person who comes into Harvest will have a minimum of three warm welcomes. So, start by recruiting happy, smiling faces to serve as greeters, and strategically place them around your campus. (Let the grumpies of your congregation serve somewhere else.)

Not only do we have trained greeters, but we have tried intentionally to develop a culture of friendliness. Go ahead and deputize every member as an unofficial greeter. Be nice. People like it.

The next step is to be sure that the church has clear directional signage. Where should people park? How do they get to the nursery? Where is the coffee? Don't forget the bathrooms.

In children's settings leaders need to be ready to engage in friendly and reassuring ways so that parents feel confident about leaving their children in your care. When parents return, thank them for the opportunity to know their children, and then send each child a postcard during the week to help establish a relationship between the leader and the child. You may also want to give new families a gift bag with information about your ministries and something fun like a bouncy ball. Who doesn't love a bouncy ball? (We used to give a giant Pixy Stix, but they got the kids all hyped on sugar. We had to rethink that one.)

In worship, make sure that the service is relevant, engaging, and biblical. Keep the pace flowing, and take notice of the volume and quality of your music. Remember, many people's greatest fears are speaking in public and being in a crowd, so don't single out your guests and ask them to stand and introduce themselves. Instead, ask your members to welcome the guests seated around them. Put the responsibility on your people, not your guests. As discussed in chapter 4, by providing excellence in the areas of children's ministry, music, preaching, and atmosphere you can almost guarantee that your guests will have a positive experience.

Later in the "Tools" part, we offer a thorough explanation of our communication card. This card gives you what you need to begin a process that thanks people for attending your church, asks them to share their first impression, and then invites them to return. In the first-time attendee letter we include a coupon that can be redeemed for a free copy of Andy Stanley's book *How Good Is Good Enough?* (Sisters, Ore.: Multnomah, 2003) on their next visit. Second-time attendees receive a letter and a coupon for a free Harvest worship CD. In addition to the letter, we send them an e-mail of welcome.

For people to stick in your church, they need relationships and responsibilities. If they don't find both of these in the first six months, they will probably fall away. Make it easy for people to join ministry teams, and give them plenty of opportunities to meet friends through community groups. Help your guests change their pronouns. People have found their church home when they begin to say "we" and "my" instead of "they" and "your." The pronouns tell the story. Once people are saying "my" and "our," they are home.

The healthiest way to grow your church is through first-time professions of faith. In order to have people accept Christ you have to have some unsaved people in the pews. When you do, never overlook the opportunity to invite unsaved people into a relationship with Jesus. At the end of every service we say something like this: "In just a moment we're going to pray together. If you've never stepped across the line to make Jesus Christ your Savior, your boss, the CEO of your life, then I want you to do that today. I'm going to say a prayer. You don't have to say anything out loud. Just pray in your heart, and if you mean business, God will hear you. Would you pray with me: Dear Jesus, as much as I know how, I put my trust in you. I still have a lot of questions, but I ask you to forgive me of my sins and help me start fresh. I believe what you did on the cross is for me, and I receive your love and forgiveness. Please help me. Amen."

We then ask people who prayed that prayer for the first time to let us know by marking the appropriate box on their communication cards. On Monday, our community group staff person calls to congratulate them and to invite them to join a group. We also send a letter to welcome them to the family of God and suggest some next steps in their spiritual journey. This letter includes a coupon for a Bible that can be picked up in our Resource Center. When they present that coupon, we have another opportunity to celebrate their faith decision.

Inviting people to the party is a great first step, but you have to be sure you're ready when they arrive. Create a system to turn first-time guests into fully devoted followers of Christ.

QUESTIONS AND THOUGHTS TO CONSIDER

1. What is our greeting process?

2. Is our signage clear for guests to follow?

3. How can we collect first-impression responses?

4. How clear is our invitation to receive Christ? How often do we do this?

5. Check out Nelson Searcy's book *Fusion* (Regal, 2006) for more on assimilation.

On the next pages, see our letters to visitors and to those newly committed to Christ.

HARVESTCHURCH
A UNITED METHODIST CONGREGATION

Hey _____!

It was really good to have you at Harvest for the first time this week. I hope you enjoyed the service. I don't know if you're looking for answers, a church home, or just passing through the area. Whatever the case, I'm glad you chose to check us out.

We think church should be a fun and practical place to get the answers we need for life. Helping people connect with Jesus is what Harvest is all about. So on your next visit, please stop by the information desk and pick up a complimentary copy of *How Good Is Good Enough?* by Andy Stanley.

As a first-time guest, you have a special point of view that we value. What was your *first impression*? Would you take a minute to fill out the enclosed postcard and drop it in the mail? We want Harvest to have a warm and comfortable atmosphere for our guests so your input will really help.

You might want to check out our website for more information about what we believe and where we are going. There's a button to e-mail us there too.

www.harvestchurch4u.org

Have a great week and we hope you can join us again soon!

478.923.8822 ° 478.332.6640 (FAX)
2322 US Hwy 41N ° Byron, GA 31008
Harveschurch4u.org

Hey _____ !

I'm so glad you've decided to commit your life to Christ! Congratulations! When we put our faith in Jesus, we become "born again." This is a term Jesus used. You are literally born in a new way . . . your first birth was physical (just ask your mom!). This time you are born in a spiritual way. It means you have a brand-new relationship with God. Now you are his child—you've been adopted!

One of the purposes that God has for his children is to become more like Jesus:

> For from the very beginning God decided that those who come to him . . . should become like his Son. (Rom. 8:29 TLB)

I know that sounds like a pretty tall order, but don't worry, God is really going to do most of the work. It's our job to cooperate, obey, and let him.

You may be asking yourself, *Now what do I do?* Let me give you a couple of suggestions.

Get involved in a good church.

Read the Bible. This is our instruction manual. I recommend a modern translation that is easy to understand. There are some great study Bibles with explanation notes.

Pray. Just talk to God like you would to a friend. It might feel awkward at first, but the more you do it, the more comfortable you'll feel.

Join a community group (Bible study). One of the best ways to learn is with other people on the same journey.

I'm really excited with you and I really want to help.

Sincerely,

Pastor Jim

P.S. We have a special gift book for you. Please bring the enclosed card and stop by the Resource Center next week and pick it up.

20

Start Tapping Volunteers

*All of you together are the one body of Christ and
each one of you is a separate and necessary part of it.*
—*1 Corinthians 12:27 TLB*

To grow your church, you are going to need help. It's great to add staff as you are able, but you will never be able to afford all the help you need. Most of the ministry in your church is going to be done through volunteers. God planned it this way. It would be a shame for only professional people to experience the joys of investing in God's work. Just think of all the personalities, gifts, and abilities we would miss if only paid people were serving. As leaders, we have the responsibility to help every attendee find a way to plug in and use his or her talents to make a difference.

If the idea of recruiting volunteers has been a pain in the past, you are not alone. We want to help you get rid of the mind-set of recruiting for a task and switch to the idea of inviting to a team. Recruiting sounds like work; inviting is a privilege. People want to be needed. Even more than that, they want to spend their lives doing something significant.

Don't ask people to do a job; instead, invite them to join you in changing the world. See the difference? For example, the parking team doesn't just maximize parking spaces. That team is the first to offer a friendly greeting to people coming onto the campus. Our children's registration team doesn't just guide children to the age-appropriate class. They have the privilege of welcoming each family warmly and assuring parents that as they worship, their children will be safe, loved, and taught God's principles. Changing our mind-set here makes a life-changing difference. Developing a strategy to build strong volunteer teams is essential. In most churches, leaders try to fill positions through appeals in the bulletin or from the pulpit. As you probably already know, this approach is not very effective. What does work is "tapping." One person already involved in ministry comes alongside someone else, gently taps him on the shoulder, and invites him to join the team and observe what's going on. No long-term commitments, just a tap and an invitation.

Once tapping becomes part of your church DNA, it will produce volunteers exponentially. Every summer the men of our church go on a retreat we call "Man Camp." It has become a tradition that men serving in various ministries take a few minutes to share what their ministry involvement has meant in their lives. It's exciting to hear the passion flowing out of these guys as they share about everything from security to puppets. Over the next few days, these same guys begin to tap their friends and invite them to join their teams. It has been tremendously successful in getting the men of our congregation engaged in service.

Here are some tips to help with tapping:

1. Never ask for help. This sounds counterintuitive, but asking for help doesn't work. As we mentioned earlier, appeals from the stage and in the bulletin aren't effective because they sound desperate. Instead of begging, try tapping and inviting.

2. Invite people to join your teams on a trial basis. It's in everyone's best interest to allow people to try things out for a while before making a commitment. We allow people to leave a ministry quickly and gracefully if it's not a good fit.

3. Help people find their SHAPE. SHAPE is an acronym coined by Rick Warren that helps people find their spiritual gifts, heart, abilities, personality, and experiences and put those to work in ministry. Developing a system within your church to help people discover their unique SHAPE will aid in plugging them in where they will be most fulfilled and fruitful. Erik Rees's book *S.H.A.P.E.* (Grand Rapids: Zondervan, 2006) may be helpful in developing your volunteer placement process.

4. Establish job requirements. Everybody can serve somewhere, but certain jobs require special screening. For instance, in children's ministry, after the tap but before on-the-job training, a background check and a safety procedure class are required. To fold bulletins on the weekdays, on the other hand, you don't even have to be a Christian. Establish and communicate clear expectations and prerequisites for each area of ministry.

5. Train on the job. Don't make the training process too complicated. Simple systems are usually effective. Allow people to observe and then discuss what happened. Then allow them to serve while you observe, and offer feedback. If all goes well, cut them loose to serve with appropriate supervision and evaluations.

6. Promote for excellence. Look for people who do things well. Remember, Jesus teaches us that those who can be trusted to do small things well can be trusted to take on more (Matt. 25:23).

7. Value your volunteers. Most volunteers also have jobs, families, and other commitments, so wise leaders encourage their teams regularly and help each member feel valued. Be

creative and find ways to celebrate people and their contributions. Some churches do this elaborately, but honestly, we have found that a pat on the back with a good "attaboy" goes a long way.

8. Hire slowly. It's always easier to get in than out of situations. Look for high-capacity volunteers who not only share your church values but also are winsome and attract others to their ministry teams. Remember to value character, chemistry, and competency as you look for your next staff person.

QUESTIONS AND THOUGHTS TO CONSIDER

1. How many people are now engaged as volunteers?

2. How effective is our current volunteer placement process?

3. What systems need to be in place to begin tapping?

4. Do we have a clear list of prerequisites for each ministry (children, finance, security, and so on)?

5. How can we express appreciation to people currently serving?

6. For more on this topic, check out *Simply Strategic Volunteers* by Tim Stevens and Tony Morgan (Loveland, Colo.: Group, 2005).

PART FIVE

<u>Tools</u>

When we go to seminars, which we do frequently, we enjoy leadership tips and inspirational motivation for worship, growth, and financial management. What we really want to leave with, though, are a few valuable tools. Tools are practical and usually can make you more effective immediately. We love that!

We have a great friend who is a master carpenter. He was building a fort for our son a few years ago and showed us some of his tools. Not just a basic hammer and saw, they were very impressive. However, we had no idea how to use them. We were glad he was building the fort because we would have made a mess of things. Good tools are awesome, but for a tool to work you need to know what it's for and how to use it. These chapters address both.

These particular tools have been so successful for us that we have nicknamed them the "magic bullets." We think they will do the same for you. Put them in your toolbox, and watch how God can use them!

21

Start Using Communication Cards

Be sure you know the condition of your flocks,
give careful attention to your herds. —Proverbs 27:23 NIV

When I, Jen, was growing up, my brother and I played a game on Sunday mornings using the registration pew pad. The pads were passed down the pew each week, and people were supposed to fill out their names and addresses and prayer concerns. Fortunately for us, our church published each week's list of visitors, as recorded in the pads, in the next week's bulletin. So, we made it a challenge to make up names and see if we could get them past the church secretary. We listed names like Ben and Eileen Dover, Barbie Cue, Scott Lanyard, and Colden Rainey. We knew few people were really filling out those things, so we figured this was a fun way to keep it interesting.

The goal of the pew pad is registration of visitors and members. But it does not allow people to share prayer concerns in a confidential manner and does not offer the opportunity to respond to the message through a profession of faith or practical next steps. As an alternative to the pew pad, try the communication card.

125

The communication card is a magic bullet in the world of ministry. Every week we include in our program a little card similar to the one you will find in this chapter. We ask everyone in attendance, members and guests, to fill one out and place it in the basket as it is passed down the row at the end of the service. The information gathered from this card is incredibly valuable and confidential. Let's take a look at what's included on this card:

1. Basic Information

This includes name, e-mail, address, phone, and a place to let us know about attendance status. This information is collected and saved in our network. Name and e-mail are the first two items on the card. We know that people don't always take time to fill out all the blanks. Keep the card simple, and ask for the information you want most first because people often fill in only two or three blanks. We also ask how they heard about the church so that we will know the most effective forms of advertising.

On the front of the card, we also have a place to mark if people are first- or second-time guests. These people get a special e-mail from the church on Monday morning and a letter from the pastor during the week, welcoming them to the church.

2. Prayer Concerns

Most of the back is left blank so that attendees can share their prayer concerns with the staff and prayer team. It is amazing what people are willing to share with us every week: information about addictions, affairs, repentance, and convictions. We make sure the crowd knows that these concerns will be kept confidential and that our goal is to partner with them through prayer. It also alerts us to someone who is in crisis so that we can step in and help immediately.

3. Next Steps

The upper left-hand corner is reserved for next steps. Every week attendees are challenged to take at least one practical next step that will apply the message in their lives. Next steps might include:

- This week, I will memorize Psalm 100.

- Today, I will share my addiction issue with a trusted friend.

- This week, I will join a community group.

- This month, I will read through the New Testament.

- This week, I will not curse or lose my temper.

- For the next three months, I will take the tithe challenge.

4. Registration for Church Events

The communication card is also an effective means of RSVP. Attendees can register for the membership class, join a community group, or volunteer for a ministry by checking a box. It gives people an easy way to let us know that they are interested, and it saves time and money in the long run.

5. Professions of Faith

As of this writing, more than two thousand people have accepted Christ at Harvest Church. How do we know that? Because we have their cards! We have been able to follow up with each of them through a letter and a personal phone call because they have given us that information on their cards. This alone makes the card a valuable tool.

Here are tips to make the communication card process more successful:

- Gather them after the message. It is critical to give people a time to respond after the sermon, especially in regard to making a profession of faith. This may mean moving your collection time around in your order of worship. It is worth it!

- Plan the follow-up process carefully. How will the cards be collected and processed? Who will see the sensitive information they may contain? Will confidentiality be an issue among the church staff?

- Don't ask for information you are not prepared to handle. For instance, don't ask people to volunteer if there is no one to ready to contact them on Monday morning.

- Have your members model this process by turning in a card every week, even if the card just has a name and e-mail on it. Having everyone turn in a card doesn't make newcomers feel self-conscious because they will see that it is standard practice.

- Refer to the card at the end of the message. Remind people to fill out their concerns, and then walk them through next steps as well as the opportunity to receive Christ. Ask them to mark the decisions they are making so that you can follow up with them for guidance and encouragement.

Another tremendous benefit of the card is that it gives the pastor and staff insight into the needs of the people. Themes often emerge as we read and study the cards. To meet people at their deepest points of need, we develop messages around presenting issues such as debt, marriage, addiction, conflict resolution, parenting, and forgiveness. The communication card also helps us know what types of Bible studies need to be offered.

A simple first step might be to leave out the weekly next steps and produce generic cards. This can be done inexpensively through a local office supply or printing company. The pew pad is a traditional tool used in many churches. However, it probably does not effectively gather the information you desire. Try the communication card instead. It is a more strategic and confidential tool for your people to use.

QUESTIONS AND THOUGHTS TO CONSIDER

1. How effective is our current registration tool?

2. What are the primary benefits of the communication card for our church?

3. What would be needed to try the communication card for a three-month trial?

4. Who will be responsible for production?

5. How will we handle follow-up to the cards?

HARVEST CHURCH
A UNITED METHODIST CONGREGATION

January 21 & 22, 2012

1st-time Guests,
Please pick up your FREE gift at
the Information Desk in the Lobby.

☐ New Contact Information

Name:
Email:
Address:
City:
State: Zip:
Best Contact Phone:

☐ 1st time guest
☐ 2nd time guest
☐ Regular Attender
☐ Member

*If you are a 1st or 2nd time guest,
how did you hear about Harvest?*

Please place this card in the offering basket at the end of the service.

Prayer Requests:

My Next Steps:
☐ Please sign me up to be baptized.
☐ Sign me for CLASS 101
☐ I will attend the Harvest Kathleen Campus during the month of February at 10:15.

1st Time Commitment:
☐ Today, for the first time, I accept God's gift of forgiveness and ask Jesus Christ to be my Savior.

www.harvestchurch4u.org

22

Stop
Using
Flannelboard

*From the tribe of Issachar . . . these men understood the
signs of the times and knew the best course for Israel to take.*
—1 Chronicles 12:32 NLT

Recently, in a Bible study we asked the students to turn to Ephesians in their Bibles. In a group of twenty-four kids, only two had a book. The rest got out their phones and scrolled to the verse. We live in a world of screens. Yet some of our churches still approach ministry with a flannelboard mind-set, comfortable with techniques invented for a previous era. How can we access more screens? Computers, smartphones, and tablets are screens that people access daily. To ignore the advantages of technology is to do a disservice to the people in our congregations and especially to those who do not yet know Christ. Like the two hundred men of Issachar, we need to understand the times we live in and wisely use the resources at our disposal.

Consider these tactics for improving your technological savvy:

WEB PRESENCE

Start with a great website. According to faithHighway, a Christian Web development company, almost 85 percent of first-time church visitors will check out a church online before actually attending. First impressions are now made online instead of in person, so your Web presence becomes increasingly important.

Go online and check out larger church websites. Survey home pages and internal pages, noting what you like and don't like. How easily is the site navigated? Does the site appear interesting? Can you relate to the pictures? Take note of format, children's ministries, directional information, service times, and style. A great website can be pricey if you hire an outside company, but there are less expensive options available that are preformatted. Many middle school kids are required to create a Web page in computer class, so you can find some people to help. But here is a word of caution: don't go generic. Select a style that represents who you are and expresses the vision of your congregation.

For instance, Harvest is a multicultural church with a casual atmosphere, a dynamic children's program, and a rock style of music. We want our website to reflect this so that people know what to expect before they drive onto the campus. This helps alleviate people's fears of facing the unknown.

We also archive messages online through our website for several purposes:

1. People can check out the style of music and teaching in advance.

2. Our deployed service people can remain connected to their church family while stationed overseas.

3. Topics can be revisited as needs arise in life (debt, anger, marriage, and so on).

APPS

Another tool that costs nothing is the free online set of resources available through open.lifechurch.tv. Craig Groeschel and the people of LifeChurch.tv have made their online Bible, YouVersion, available to everyone using a now popular phone app. Through this same app, churches can integrate live tools. Currently at Harvest, we use the YouVersion in three ways: (1) a Bible study, (2) sermon notes used during the live event, and (3) a parents' tool for sharing what children are learning weekly in their settings.

SOCIAL MEDIA

Many pastors and churches use Twitter, blogging, and YouTube extensively. Facebook is a great vehicle for posting music, announcements, and short videos that people can use to spread your message virally.

VIDEO

Video is another form of technology that is particularly effective in worship. We love to share prerecorded, well-edited testimonies. Notice the caveats: prerecorded and well edited. If you do not have the staff or volunteers to pull this off within your congregation, check out inexpensive, professionally done videos available through sites like worshiphousemedia.com and sermonspice.com. Video can upgrade a good message to great for little expense.

E-MAIL / TEXT

For maintaining clear lines of communication with your church members, mass e-mail, through a service like ConstantContact.com, and texting are viable options. However, people under the age of thirty do not tend to be fans of e-mail. Facebook and text are usually better means of reaching them.

ONLINE GIVING

Provide people an online option to give. Currently, more than 40 percent of the giving in our church is done online. We, personally, are old school and still write a check, but it is one of only about six checks we write a month. Our financial world is increasingly paperless. Make it easy for your people to give to your church.

If technology is not your thing, don't be discouraged. Instead, be tenacious and surround yourself with people who can take you to the next level. Technology is a moving target because upgrades occur so rapidly. Stay ahead of the curve in order to use today's tools to reach today's generation. The benefits are greater than we can even imagine.

Recently while greeting people in the lobby, we met a new family from North Pole, Alaska. As we introduced ourselves, they said, "Jim, Jen, we know you. We've been worshiping with you for months online. It's good to finally be here in person." We're not sure exactly where North Pole is, but it is a long way from Middle Georgia. This family had found their new church months in advance of their move through our website and online services. They seemed to feel at home in a place in which they had never been physically; through technology and through worship, we were like old friends to them.

Start leveraging technology for God's kingdom!

QUESTIONS AND THOUGHTS TO CONSIDER

1. Is our website maintained in an engaging style with current information?

2. Does our Web presence reflect who we are as a congregation?

3. How might we use Facebook to invite people into our doors?

4. What tools can we put in place immediately?

5. With whom can we consult for more information on technology and its many uses in our local setting?

23

Start Counting

Get the facts at any price. —Proverbs 23:23 TLB

Gathering accurate information will help you and the leaders of your congregation take a good look at exactly where you are and then help direct you where you need to go next. Surprisingly, church leaders at many congregations seem out of touch with their situation. How can you get where you want to go if you don't really know where you are? Get the facts. Accurate information is a key element of successful leadership. King Solomon knew this truth three thousand years ago: "Be sure you know the condition of your flocks, give careful attention to your herds" (Prov. 27:23 NIV).

Here are basic questions that key leaders should ask and have the answers at their fingertips:

1. How many people accepted Christ in our church last month?

2. What is our average attendance?

3. How many children attend?

4. How many first-time guests have visited in the past month?

5. How many of our parking spaces are empty?

6. What is our weekly, monthly, and annual giving?

7. How many people are in a small group?

Keeping accurate records is critical. When we do, we take out the guesswork and get to the truth of our situation. Every Monday morning our staff receives a stat sheet of the weekend services. This sheet includes how many people attended each service, how many volunteers were available for each service, how full the parking lot was, how many people made a decision for Christ, how many people asked to be plugged into a ministry, how many want to join a community group, and so on. From these sheets we are able to chart trends and make clear decisions.

By studying the data of our situation, we make informed decisions, such as when to add staff, how to advertise, how to support struggling ministry areas, and when to add a new service. Because we know how many people we serve, we know when to add children's workers, greeters, or even chairs. Good stats lead to good decisions.

If you are in a small church, you may be thinking, *We don't need to keep up with all of this.* Yes, you do. The truth about growth or decline can be subtle. Often by the time you realize what's going on, it is difficult to change the negative momentum. Also, the numbers get you past how people feel to the truth of the situation. Regardless of your size or the way you may think things are going, accurate statistics give an impartial reflection of reality.

A great leader always asks questions and searches for the truth. You must find the truth before the truth finds you in the form of a crisis or major problem. Recently, we met with another church staff. As they shared their struggles, it became obvious within the first few minutes that they had a very serious issue. Their attendance was in steady decline, from 550 down to 350 in just two years. When we asked about children's ministries, the senior staff members were sketchy and threw out a vague guesstimate of about seventy kids a week. But another staff person with small children said, "Actually, we only have about thirty children each weekend, and if more come, there would be no room for them." Parents were not comfortable leaving their children in such a crowded environment, and that fear had been affecting church attendance. It was a major issue affecting their growth, but it was not even on their radar. The truth had found them before they found it.

Keeping accurate records can help you stay on top of the truth of your situation. By charting numbers such as first-time visitors and decisions for Christ, we can measure our effectiveness in reaching new people. By keeping up with capacity issues, we can know when to add another service or make an addition. These numbers also tell us when we are in a 911 situation. A 911 situation means we need help. It's time to call the EMT—emergency ministry technician. In other words, a consultant.

At Harvest, we hire outside consultants about every two years. They come in and help us look with new eyes at the health of our church. Before they even come into town, they ask for the numbers. Nothing is out of bounds: salaries, worship style, finances, structure, staffing, landscape, and children's ministry. They bring an objective perspective that clarifies our situation. In just a day or two, it is amazing that these consultants can study our situation and give us such clear insight about next steps. Record keeping is key to that process.

We must face the brutal facts in our churches. In the United States, we are losing ground. We can sugarcoat the numbers. But the truth is that the church in America is in trouble. It may not be dying, but it is sick. If one of us were to become ill, the other would do absolutely everything within our power to find out what was wrong and figure out how to fix it, including taking a leave of absence from the job, quitting hobbies, using our savings, or doing whatever it took. Church, Jesus is counting on us to love others in that same desperate way. We know you already know this because you've read the Great Commandment. But we want it to sink in, in fresh new ways for you; the world around us is sick, and we need to find ways to inject the vaccine of Christ's love into its veins.

It's exciting to be able to share that more than two thousand people have accepted Christ at Harvest Church in the past ten years. But that's not just a number. That's about people. We have their communication cards with their names, e-mails, and addresses. We have been able to follow up with them because we kept those records. We know who these people are and on what day they received Christ. How? We carefully gather and value that information.

We did not see as much growth in 2011 as we did in 2010. Although we still have a large crowd, our growth has slowed. We're still seeing many first- and second-time guests. We're still seeing people accept Jesus weekly. But by keeping records, we discovered the hard truth that not as many of the new believers get plugged into community groups as we'd like. This information helps our Christian education team know how to focus for the future. Without the statistical data, we probably would not now be addressing this issue of retention.

Last, it is wise to gather the facts regarding unchurched people in your area. The U.S. Census Bureau and your local chamber of commerce can help you gather the data. At Harvest, we intentionally try to attract unchurched families who have school-age children still living at home. These are good people, but they have not found Jesus to be relevant in their lives. So, we want to know what radio stations they listen to, what television shows they watch, what they read, and what they perceive as their greatest needs. We want to do what Paul did when he said, "I have become all things to all people so that by all possible means I might save some" (1 Cor. 9:22 NIV). We do the research. We learn about our targets, and then we structure our advertising, music style, and worship to reach them. Guess what? It works!

QUESTIONS AND THOUGHTS TO CONSIDER

1. What information do we keep faithfully?

2. What information do we need?

3. What facts do we need to face as a congregation?

4. What system is needed to gather and organize critical data?

Simplifed Statistical Sheet

Weekend Services	Sunday				Date:
Attendance	1st Service 9:00am	2nd Service 10:30am	3rd Service 12noon	Subtotal	Total
Worship Attendance					
Volunteers & Others					
Children Leaders					Difference from
Children Attendance					previous week:
Subtotal by Service					

Giving

Tithes & Offerings				

Communication Cards

Professions of Faith			
Ist Time Visitors			
2nd Time Visitors			
Plug in to Ministry			
Join a Community Group			

Capacities

	#		
% Chairs Filled	0		
% Parking Spaces Filled	0		

How Visitors Found Us

Family / Friends	Billboard	Magnet / Decal	Postcard / Mailer	Facebook / Web	TV Commercial

24

Start Confronting Gossip

Fire goes out without wood,
and quarrels disappear when gossip stops.
—Proverbs 26:20 NLT

Within the Harvest family we have a saying: "We don't do that here." This statement covers a variety of issues, including talking badly about other churches, whining, being mean, and allowing non-tithers to handle church money. At the top of the "we don't do that here" list is gossip! Proverbs 16:28 (NLT) states, "Gossip separates the best of friends." It also destroys the best of churches.

Gossip in the church can take many forms. Most commonly, we see it in the form of closed-door conversations or critical comments made at the expense of someone else. Sometimes it's called a prayer request. It might go something like this: "We need to pray for the Smiths. I heard they were filing for bankruptcy. We also need to pray for Peggy. She's pregnant again, and she can't even handle the kids she's already got!" Gossip is hurtful, even if it happens to be true. As a spiritual leader, you cannot allow it to continue.

We began Harvest with just our little family of four. As we shared the vision, others joined us, and in the first year our attendance grew to about 150. We were thankful for each of them. However, one particular family had an issue with gossip. They were working hard in ministries. They were even reaching out to us personally as friends, but behind the scenes, word kept getting back to us that they had a lot to say about, well, basically everything. So, I, Jim, took the husband to lunch and confronted the issue. The conversation was gentle, but direct, and I gave specifics about what was not acceptable. I encouraged the husband to address the issue at home, and I let him know that I'd help him any way I could. I thought the lunch went well. Apparently, he didn't. He and his wife got mad and loudly left the church. (You've probably experienced something similar. It's painful.) We lost a lot of sleep over it, but then about a month later, a new family began attending. When Jen asked what brought them to Harvest, they said, "We know the family that Jim confronted, and they told us what Jim said to them about the gossip situation. We've been listening to them gossip for years, and we decided that we wanted to be a part of a church that would not allow it to continue." It was never mentioned again, but the family that joined us has been an integral part of the church ever since.

As a leader, you get to decide the atmosphere of your church. What is acceptable behavior? Don't allow this to be determined casually or to erode over time. Instead, establish clear biblical expectations of behavior. Once these expectations are clearly communicated and enforced, you will be amazed at how quickly those expectations become the norm of behavior.

Years ago I, Jen, worked in a United Methodist mission setting with impoverished children. Some days I had as many as a hundred kids show up after school for an afternoon Bible lesson and games. Occasionally, I had a helper, but most days it was just the kids and me for two hours. These children came from very tough situations. Most of them had not experienced a lot of love and had very little structure in their lives. So, from the very beginning I had to establish clear guidelines about what behavior was okay and what was not. No hitting, cursing, name-calling, and so on. When a child had a bad day and broke one of the rules, I would just say, "It's time to go home today. Remember, we don't do that here. But I'll see you tomorrow, and we'll try again." That child would then leave without an after-school snack. In three years, I sent only two children home. Why did it work? First, I loved those kids, and they knew it. Second, they knew I was serious about enforcing the guidelines. The same thing works with adults.

One of our early ministry mentors told us to "run to conflict." Doing this doesn't come naturally for us or most people we know in ministry. In general, ministry leaders are nice people, and that is a good thing. But just playing nice and allowing sin to continue around you is a horrible leadership failure. There will be times when you absolutely must run to conflict because to ignore it offers a silent stamp of approval.

Another principle to use in conflict resolution comes from Jesus: "If another believer sins against you, go privately and point out the offense" (Matt. 18:15 NLT). Let's say John has a problem with Bob. When you hear John complain about Bob, address it immediately. Ask John if he has gone to Bob and discussed the situation. If not, walk John personally to Bob and say, "Hey, Bob, John here would like to talk with you." Then step away. If Bob is not available at that time, then say, "I'll tell Bob that you need to talk to him so that you can address this directly with him." When you employ the Matthew 18 principle, at least three things are likely to happen:

1. People will quit telling you their petty gripes.
2. Instead of gossip, issues will be handled directly by the involved parties.
3. Complaining, in general, will decrease dramatically.

So how do you communicate your "we don't do that here" list? You do it directly and nicely in various settings. In our membership class, in small groups, in leadership training, and especially from the stage, we let our people know that being part of the church family is a privilege that comes with responsibility. Part of that responsibility is living above reproach. We then address several common issues with which people in our community struggle, such as abusing alcohol, living together outside marriage, cursing, lying, engaging in mean-tempered exchanges, and, yes, even gossiping. At first this may feel uncomfortable, but that's okay. Don't back away from high standards.

As leaders, we have the responsibility to communicate clearly not just what the church does but how we do it. Create a culture in your setting where people can kindly address situations and gently say, "Remember, we don't do that here." You'll be amazed at how powerful this simple strategy is!

Remember, people are going to leave your church. Determining what is and is not acceptable in your setting allows you to have a lot of say about who that will be. We had hoped that the gossiping family would stay at Harvest, but not if they continued what they were doing. We don't do that here.

QUESTIONS AND THOUGHTS TO CONSIDER

1. How has gossip affected our church recently?

2. What does our "we don't do that here" list look like?

3. What would we like it to be?

4. How will we communicate it?

5. How can we employ the Matthew 18 principle among our staff, leaders, and congregation?

25

Stop Allowing Staff to Drain the Church

He who walks with the wise grows wise,
but a companion of fools suffers harm.
—Proverbs 13:20 NIV 1984

We like the people on our staff. In fact, some of them are more like family than friends. However, many pastors and church staff would not be able to echo this sentiment.

Life is short. Choose carefully with whom you spend it. The right staff people make average leaders great. On the other hand, average or mismatched staff drain great leaders. Additionally, poor staffing can drain your church spiritually, emotionally, and financially. So choose your team carefully. This also applies to your leadership teams, who are basically volunteer staff members.

Here are practical suggestions that may assist you in the area of staffing:

HIRE POSITIVE, ENCOURAGING LEADERS

We were given this advice years ago: "You should want to do life with the people that you hire." In fact, he went so far as to say that you should want to have lunch with them on a regular basis. If you don't, your people probably don't, either. And that's a problem.

The staff of your church represent Christ to the world. Ministry is just as much about the messenger as it is the message. So be careful who your messengers are. The paid and unpaid leaders of your church should be positive, encouraging people with magnetic personalities. If they aren't, it's time for attitude adjustments.

HIRE PEOPLE WHO REPRODUCE THEMSELVES

When you hire someone to do a job, you have added one person to your ministry team. When you hire someone to lead a job, you have added teams of people to your ministry. There is a huge difference.

Our worship leader is not hired to sing and lead the music. She is on staff to organize and deliver a quality worship experience that coordinates with the weekend message and to recruit people to accomplish this. This may or may not include her being on the stage. Additionally, she oversees the development of the website, audio and video teams, church marketing, and set design. How can one person possibly do this? She does it through ministry teams. Her job is to recruit, train, and encourage these teams. Through team leadership, she is able to put dozens of people into ministry each week and reproduce herself exponentially.

By the same token, our office staff is not paid to produce, collate, and distribute weekly materials. Instead, their role is to recruit and organize a team of laity. Essentially, key leaders, both hired and volunteer, are in place to reproduce themselves. A good hire is a person who multiplies ministry in his or her area of expertise. This is not only biblical; it proves to be great stewardship.

HIRE FROM WITHIN WHEN POSSIBLE

Someone serving in your church may be your next great staff member.

146

The people serving in your church already understand and embrace the mission and values of your congregation. Outsiders take as long as several years to adapt to your culture and unique DNA, which gives insiders an advantage as new staff members.

Some of our staff were hired because they were doing such effective jobs of leading teams of volunteers that we felt really guilty not paying them. Basically, they were already staff. We just needed to do the right thing and pay them for their long hours. By giving volunteers increasing amounts of responsibility, you can grow your staff through those who continue to rise to the tasks in front of them.

HIRE ADMINISTRATORS FIRST

Our student ministry is run by a wonderful woman who is also a full-time nurse practitioner. She loves teenagers and does a great job interacting with them. We hired her because she can administrate a team of leaders.

Instead of hiring a traditional youth director, we opted to add an administrator to the team who could organize a team of small-group networks throughout our region. Weekly, more than three hundred students gather in homes for fellowship, Bible study, outreach programs, and prayer. Our staff person's primary role is to recruit, train, and resource those small-group leaders. Her job involves Christian education, but at its core it is an administrative job of organizing and deploying leaders.

When you have to choose, go for administrative skills over charisma. The payoff appears in the multiplication process.

HIRE BASED ON THE THREE C'S OF THE CHURCH

If you Google the three C's of hiring, you will get a plethora of responses. Critical thinking, communication, credentials, compensation, and other responses appear. But within the church, we like the three C's that stand for character, chemistry, and competence, in that order.

Character. You can't get around bad character. The staff of your church must live above reproach. You absolutely cannot ignore or cover up deficiencies in this area. As part of the hiring process, do the background work necessary to find out with whom you are working. All too often, we hire people for what they can do, but we end up firing them for who they are.

At Harvest, we require every staff person to sign and live by a code of ethics. This covenant addresses financial decisions, tithing, sexual conduct, lying, gossip, and alcohol and drug use. People are going to mess up in life. But when the "mess up" is a major moral failure, you have to address it immediately.

Character also involves just plain being a nice person. If you have staff members who don't play well with others, you need to decide how long you'll allow it to continue.

Chemistry. There are times when even good Christian people just don't get along well together. We're nice. They're nice. But we happen to be allergic to one another. Just because you happen to be allergic to peanuts doesn't mean that they're bad nuts. However, it does mean that you don't need to be around peanut butter. Another common thing that causes allergies is ragweed. When chemistry isn't good, staff members can become the ragweed of the church and cause a huge drain on leaders and the church. These are difficult situations because no one has really done anything wrong. It's just a bad match.

Be honest and loving about the situation. Help such staff members find a place, even if it's not in your setting, where their gifts and personalities can be appreciated and where they can flourish.

Competence. If the church is taking money out of the tithes and offerings to pay a salary, that job needs to be done well. Staff members should be expected not only to have good attitudes but also to do their tasks with excellence. Job expectations should be clear and evaluated on a regular basis. Offer training to help staff increase their skill set when appropriate. But at the end of the day, if the job is not getting done, leaders must address the issue and put people in place who can help achieve the mission of the church.

HIRE ON A TRIAL BASIS AND THEN EVALUATE

We have established the practice of hiring someone on a ninety-day contract and evaluating how things are going every thirty days in that period. This practice allows us to evaluate chemistry, offer the new person direction and guidance, and allow the staff person time to decide whether the position is a good fit for him or her. If all goes well during the ninety-day contract, it may be appropriate to make a permanent hire. If there are still questions, the contract can be extended for another period of time. The contractual agreement allows both parties a chance to try things out and be sure that it is going to work well. This has worked for us, but may not be right for all churches. We cannot give you legal advice, and you should check the employment laws in your area.

HIRE LOTS OF "10 FOR 10'S"

A "10 for 10" hire is someone hired for ten hours a week at ten dollars an hour. Many of our full-time people started in this capacity. Usually, we take a high-capacity volunteer and ask her or him to move to ten hours a week, which translates to only $5,200 per year. If that goes well, hours can be added in the future.

People who are high capacity, retired, or stay-at-home parents are often willing to give ten hours a week in a staff position, and often go above and beyond out of their heart for the ministry. They enjoy the significant work and bring expertise to the church that you may not be able to afford in a full-time position.

HIRE SLOWLY AND FIRE FAST!

The courtship period of the hiring process should be long and diligent. Ask hard questions. Meet often. Take prospective staff out to lunch with key leaders, and study the chemistry among them. Check the references they give you and then find some they didn't give you to be sure you have the whole story. In other words, make the engagement process nice and long.

On the other hand, when character, chemistry, or competence is not up to par, it's time to say good-bye. We believe everyone deserves a heads-up before being dismissed, with the exception of extreme moral failure. However, when attempts have been made to improve the situation, but it's not happening, good leaders make the call to let people go. Be sure you have documented the situation so that you are able to support the decision later. Again, also be aware of employment law in your area.

Remember, if you drag out the firing process, people will probably take sides, and there may be divisive damage done within the church. So, keep good records. Set clear expectations. Help people succeed when possible. But when necessary, let people go quickly.

QUESTIONS AND THOUGHTS TO CONSIDER

1. Does our staff work well as a team?

2. What is the primary expectation of staff: to do or to lead?

3. How do we communicate our code of ethics for church leadership?

4. What would the ideal staff situation look like in our setting?

5. Would I want to have lunch monthly with our staff members?

26

Start Valuing
<u>Membership</u>

So let us concentrate on the things which make for harmony,
and on the growth of one another's character.
—Romans 14:19 JBP

Most churches want to reach and attract new members. Our primary goal as believers is to love God and other people and to lead those far from God into a relationship with Jesus Christ. As believers, we want to reach new people for Christ and help them come into the family of God and grow in their faith. The first step in the process, of course, is inviting new people into the church. When that is accomplished, how do we help them explore and understand the values and direction of the congregation? And then how do we invite them into membership?

The system you develop for accepting and incorporating new members says a lot about the value you place on membership and what membership involves. Clear communication on the front end of membership is extremely important in establishing expectations and avoiding misunderstanding in the future.

The process of membership varies from church to church even within the same denomination. There are great extremes. On one end of the spectrum, the pastor may announce during the closing song that the "doors of the church are open" and anyone wanting to join may come to the front. Sometimes there are a few questions asked, but membership often simply involves walking forward and shaking the pastor's hand. In such a case, the unspoken message is that membership is not highly valued. In fact, it usually requires more commitment to join the PTA or a civic club than it does a church like this.

On the other end of the membership spectrum, there is a commitment to a lengthy membership class, sometimes up to thirty weeks! That's an extreme commitment.

We prefer to find a balance between these two approaches. Offer a one- or two-session course designed to share the primary purpose, values, and expectations with potential members. At Harvest, we have a required membership class that is offered every few months. We were introduced to the membership class system at Saddleback Church and adapted it for our denomination and specific mission. (Ironically, the concept of a membership requirement for church life predates the Baptist roots of Saddleback Church to John Wesley, the founder of Methodism. Sadly, most United Methodist churches no longer practice this concept.) It is a two-hour course that we teach together. At the end of the class, people are given an opportunity to sign the Harvest membership commitment. They then activate their membership when they choose to join a ministry team.

In the class, everyone is given a workbook, and we teach through it. We cover what it means to be a Christ follower, the history and theology of The United Methodist Church, and the mission and vision for Harvest Church in particular. This is a great time to share the DNA of your church and answer questions on a personal level. A membership class not only raises the value of membership but also communicates clearly where your church is headed.

Have you ever gotten on the wrong bus or plane? If you board a plane thinking you're going to Los Angeles and then find out the plane is headed to Boston, you would probably be aggravated. The captain would be frustrated by your mistake, and the other passengers would probably wonder what all the fuss was about. The same thing happens in churches. If you think the church is going, or should be going, in one direction but ends up somewhere else, you become frustrated. In the membership class we are very up front about how and why we do things. We lay out the benefits and expectations of membership. We want everyone to know where the plane is going. There is no bait and switch. We want people to find a church where they can put down roots, roll up their sleeves, and jump into ministry and maturity.

We love our local church. But we realize that it isn't going to be a perfect fit for everyone, maybe because of style of music, expectations, or mission focus. So, we tell people during membership class, "This is not a time-share presentation with high pressure to get you to sign up today." We'd rather they wait if they have questions. Our goal is that after hearing the Harvest DNA, they will be excited about joining the team or frustrated that it's not what they were expecting. Either way is okay because then they know what to do next.

We often say, "If the vision excites you, come on board the Harvest Church battleship! If it frustrates you, no problem. We can still be friends. But this particular church is probably not for you. There are a lot of great churches in this area. The pastors are friends of ours, and we are all on the same team. We'll be glad to help you get connected with one of them."

So, here are a few reasons to hold a membership class:

1. It Communicates Vision and Direction

The membership class is a great time to cast vision and help people know about the mission and direction of the church. We clearly state our destination and how we are going to get there. Membership classes let people know where this ship is headed so that they aren't surprised or frustrated later. The clear vision communicated in the membership class will reduce confusion and frustration in the future.

2. It Raises the Value of Membership.

People tend to rise or fall to the level of expectation you place on them. This is true in business, sports, and parenting. It's also true in the church. While on a mission trip to Central America, Jim noticed that one of his team members was missing. It turned out that this guy had left the worksite to attend a local Rotary meeting. This man later shared with the team that when he joined Rotary, he agreed to weekly meetings, and he wanted to honor that commitment, even in another country.

Most Rotary Clubs expect and require more from their members than the local church does. The same could be said of your kid's soccer team or dance company or the local PTA. Joining any of these groups requires a clear commitment, and in most cases, people keep that commitment. We need to relearn this lesson in the church.

We are the body of Christ! The church is the hope for a lost world. The church has been given a mission from Jesus to change the world. Why aren't we being more effective? It may be that we do not take the Great Commission seriously enough. As leaders, we have the responsibility to communicate clearly the privileges and the responsibilities of becoming a part of God's church.

3. It Builds Unity

Unity is always a good thing in a family, on a team, and in a church. A membership class can help everyone in your church get on the same page. Harvest is a diverse church, and we love that. Our people are black, white, Asian, and Hispanic; blue collar, white collar, and most often no collar! God loves diversity. So, with all those kinds of people with various backgrounds and baggage, how can we have unity? Easy. We have a unified vision. Every member knows the mission of Harvest, and each individual brings his or her gifts, graces, and culture to the table to help fulfill that mission. You didn't choose your family or the place you were born. But you do get to choose your church family. There's an old saying about unity: "If you are busy rowing the boat, you don't have time to rock the boat." A membership class helps you row together.

4. It Distinguishes Your Church from Secular Organizations

A lot of people in your community think the church, Rotary, Kiwanis, PTA, and Lion's Clubs are pretty much the same things: good people in good organizations, doing some nice projects to help others. There is a huge difference. The church has the message and power of Jesus Christ.

One day a man named a man we'll call "Sam" walked into the church office and asked if he could talk. He had been coming to Harvest for several months and even attended a recent membership class. "I've never really attended a church before, and I sure enjoy coming to Harvest," he said. "I have one question, though: Do you really need to be a Christian to join?"

It was a surprising question. "Uh, yeah, Sam, you do. It sounds like you may have some bigger questions than membership. The most important thing is not membership at Harvest. The most important thing is a relationship with Jesus Christ. That's why Jesus died on the cross. We built Harvest for people just like you. People who didn't grow up in church and have questions about God."

Sam's questions were eye opening for us. He went on to tell us his story: a nice guy, a retired engineer, a master gardener, and a very analytical thinker. He concluded by saying, "I sure enjoy the music and your talks. I'm just not sure what I believe about God." We assured him that he was welcome and encouraged him to keep asking those questions about God. Before Sam left the office, we gave him Lee Strobel's books *The Case for Faith* and *The Case for Christ* (Grand Rapids: Zondervan, 2005 and 2001).

A couple of weeks later Sam called the office. He was so excited on the other end of the line. "I get it now. I get it! I believe! I believe! After reading those books, all of a sudden I just realized I do believe in Jesus! He really died for me." Not long after that, Sam was baptized and joined Harvest. It was a fun baptism!

Here's a scary thought. What if, not wanting to offend Sam, we had responded, "Sam, you are such a nice guy. Come on into membership. You'll probably get it one day." And maybe he would have. But maybe he wouldn't.

People in your community need Jesus. But don't forget. People in your pews need Jesus too.

Friends, we don't want anyone ever to be able to say, "You made me a member of your church, but I never really knew Jesus for myself." You probably have people like Sam sitting in your congregation right now. They need to know that a vital relationship with Jesus is the fundamental first step to church membership.

QUESTIONS AND THOUGHTS TO CONSIDER

1. What do we expect of church members?

2. Is that clearly communicated? If so, how?

3. How would a membership class increase the unity of our congregation?

CONCLUSION
Start Now,
<u>Stop Waiting</u>

If you wait for perfect conditions, you will never get anything done.
—Ecclesiastes 11:4 NLT 1996

We have a friend who is a part-time local pastor. He serves a small country church. A good crowd on Sunday morning for him is about thirty people. When we met him, he was ready to try new things. He knew that people within driving distance of his church needed what the church alone had to offer. He began to invite people, and to his congregation's surprise, a new family with small children showed up. We know they were surprised because they had no nursery or children's leaders, and they were not prepared to welcome this family. But a week later they were. A fresh coat of paint, some new toys, and a few people ready to love on some babies were awaiting this family. This pastor started inviting, people started coming, and the church got busy. Our pastor friend is not trying to develop a megachurch in a rural setting. His dream is to be as effective as possible in the situation where he serves. That's a good and noble goal.

Another pastor we admire is a second-career pastor serving a small traditional congregation. We got to know "Bill" through a coaching network, where we saw him step out in faith to try a few new things. He started small with introducing a communication card instead of a pew pad and sending out invitations to people in the community. Bill even started a second service that he hoped would attract some of the younger families in his area. Not everyone was thrilled with Pastor Bill's new initiatives. He did them anyway. We were actually surprised at how passionately Bill began to lead, and we were concerned that he might become discouraged from lack of support. When we asked him about it, he said basically that he just couldn't wait any longer. He was getting started later in life, and time was critical. You have to love that tenacious attitude.

Pastors, stop waiting for the superpastorate. There is no perfect church filled with only encouraging, kind, tithing members waiting with potato salad to welcome you. Lay leaders, stop waiting for a superstar pastor who is thirty-five years old with forty years of experience and is witty and wise and sings only your favorite songs. Friends, it's just us. Jesus has left us here with this incredibly huge task—the Great Commission. It's just us.

We mentioned earlier that it's a healthy practice to go to the grocery store, gas station, or mall and take a look around. Really look at each of the people you find there in your community. Jesus loves them, and he died for each of them. He wants us to love them too.

Their stories may be messy. Their needs may seem overwhelming. They may be tired and short-tempered from carrying their hurts and baggage for so long. God wants us to love them. If you want to grow your church, think creatively, question your systems, work harder, challenge the status quo, but most of all, love deeply. Ask God to help you see people the way he does. Ask him to make your heart hurt for what his heart hurts. Get down on your knees, and say in advance, "Yes, God, I'll do whatever it takes to share You with these people."

That attitude will overcome many obstacles. Be friendly. Smile often. Look for the win in difficult church decisions, but don't allow the Great Commission to go undone.

We have shared many personal stories and strategies, and some of them may not work in every situation. But some of them will. Our suggestion is to begin to fast and pray and ask God to reveal a shared vision for you and your church leaders. Begin to dream about how you can adapt some of these ideas and apply them in your situation. Don't underestimate the power of the Holy Spirit in this process. But also remember that "if you wait for perfect conditions, you will never get anything done." That's practical advice from Ecclesiastes.

A couple of years ago I, Jim, was feeling down. Harvest was growing, but I was overwhelmed. I was tired and stressed. I really didn't know what to do to manage the growth or to take the church to the next level. So I prayed, but it was a bit of a whiny prayer: "Lord, Harvest is growing, but I don't know what to do next. Why don't you send Rick Warren or somebody like that here? They'd probably know what to do. I'm sure he could do a better job than me anyway." (I warned you it was whiny.)

Then I felt like God spoke to me in that still, small voice . . . loudly!

Yes, Jim, Rick could do a better job . . . but he's busy right now doing what I told him to do! And I want you to get busy doing what I've told you to do! Ouch, that one stung!

Leaders, it's just us. Like me, you may be overwhelmed with the idea of starting this and stopping that. Don't do too much at once, and don't go it alone. Begin with prayer and fasting. Work with the leaders of your church. Be winsome and pleasant in how you approach things, and then get started. If you want to see new results, you are going to have to try some new things. What will you do first?

Made in the USA
Lexington, KY
13 May 2013